WORLD WAR II POW CAMPS IN OHIO

DR. JAMES VAN KEUREN

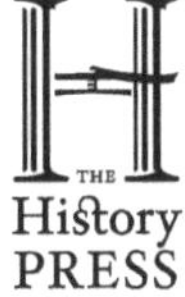

Published by The History Press
Charleston, SC
www.historypress.com

Front cover, top left: courtesy of the Ottawa County Historical Museum, Peggy Debien, curator; *top center*: courtesy of the Ottawa County Historical Museum, Peggy Debien, curator; *top right*: courtesy of NARA Photo No. SC 197675-s; *bottom*: Courtesy of the Ottawa County Historical Museum, Peggy Debien, curator.
Back cover, top: Courtesy of the Ottawa County Historical Museum, Peggy Debien, curator; *bottom*: courtesy of the Ottawa County Historical Museum, Peggy Debien, curator.

First published 2018

Manufactured in the United States

ISBN 9781467141666

Library of Congress Control Number: 2018952867

To the men and women of Camp Perry, the Erie Proving Ground and its branch camps—the home-front heroes who presided over the prisoners of war in a professional, dignified matter and whose actions can be attributed to the leadership of camp commander Lieutenant Colonel E.C. McCormick Jr. and his staff.

CONTENTS

ACKNOWLEDGEMENTS

I would like to thank my wife, Pat, for her patience and encouragement during my lengthy hours of research and writing to ensure the end product is an accurate historical summary of POW Camp Perry and its branch camps during World War II. As summer residents of Lake Erie's South Bass Island (Put-in-Bay, Ohio), we often heard islanders talk about the World War II prisoners of war housed at nearby Camp Perry. I finally decided to investigate and eventually discovered that there were more than 430,000 prisoners of war in the United States and that Camp Perry was one of the major base camps in Ohio, housing more than 6,000 Italian and German prisoners from 1943 to 1946 there and at its various branch camps.

This book includes photographs, charts and a view into the daily lives of the prisoners of war at Camp Perry, the Erie Proving Ground and its branch camps. Examples of trench art, labor contracts, German prisoners of war letters, camp newspapers, branch camp information and testimony from area residents familiar with the prisoners who worked at local farms and industries are all found in this book. Later into my research, I unearthed a hidden story—at the conclusion of World War II, the Army had left behind toxic waste in burial dumps at the properties and in Lake Erie that has cost the government millions of dollars to remediate. The work is still ongoing some seventy years later.

A special thank-you to Peggy Debien, curator at the Ottawa County Historical Museum, who allowed me to spend time at the museum gathering historical information and taking many photographs. I am also indebted to Steve Cooper, general manager and marketing manager of the North Civilian Marksmanship Program at the Camp Perry Training Site, who, like Ms. Dieben, graciously granted me large portions of his time, in addition to the modern-day overview of Camp Perry that we see in chapter 16. Other contributors who provided research include Dr. James Banks, director of the Crile Archive Center for History Education; Rick Booth, for the information detailing Fletcher General Hospital in Cambridge, Ohio; Andrew Buckman, city historian of the Andrew L. Tuttle Memorial Museum–Defiance POW Camp; Jill Ellis, office associate of the Ohio State University Extension, Mercer County–Celina POW Camp; Kay Fisher, director of Clinton County Historical Center–Wilmington POW Camp; Richard Halquist, research coordinator at the Fort Wayne History Center–Thomas A. Scott POW Camp; and, not to be outdone, the great researchers at the National Archives and Records Administration—without their assistance I would not have been able to capture the historical information archived for more than seventy years.

Another thank-you to Mark A. Walters of SandPrint Memoirs & Editing LLC, for his sharp editing of both this book and my previous title, *A Tribute to the 109th Evacuation Hospital Semi-Mobile Unit*; Bryan Miller at OfficeMax in North Olmsted for framing the photos; to Edith Herbrank, for translating the *Der Aufbau* newspapers, letters and postcard. Finally, a special thank-you to John Rodrigue and Rick Delaney of The History Press, who took me through every phase of the publication process to ensure that we had a quality product that would be appreciated by the reader.

INTRODUCTION

The United States started to receive prisoners of war in May 1942, when thirty-two German and one Japanese prisoners arrived. By May 1945, there were 425,871 prisoners housed at 511 base camps and 175 branch camps in every U.S. state except Nevada, Montana and North Dakota. The influx of the prisoners of war caught U.S. military officials unprepared to accommodate so many inmates.[1]

According to the Rand Corporation report "The Battle Behind the Wire," military officials underestimated the number of prisoners of war and the speed with which they would be received; did not realize the ideological differences between the subgroups of Germans; and were slow to recognize that there was an opportunity, through re-education programs, to shape the prisoner's mind-set for his post-conflict life.[2]

Even though there were some hostilities—including hardened Nazi prisoners of war using intimidation and censorship to control fellow prisoners—British and U.S. findings indicated that only about 10 percent of the prisoners were firmly committed to Nazism, 10 percent were opposed to it, and the remainder were political or somewhat patriotic.[3]

Camp Perry, situated three miles west of Port Clinton, Ohio, opened in 1906, when it was selected as a major base camp to improve marksmanship skills lacking during the Spanish-American War and then became a site to train soldiers during World Wars I and II. The camp also contained an artillery ordnance storage area and range called the Erie Proving Ground. Camp Perry was named after Oliver Hazard Perry, the American naval commander who won the Battle of Lake Erie during the War of 1812 and is famous for saying, "Don't give up the ship!"

The outbreak of World War II led to the conversion of Camp Perry in 1943 into a prisoner of war camp where Italian and German prisoners were housed. Camp Perry became a major labor force in northwest Ohio from 1943 to 1946 and a base camp that, along with its branch camps, housed more than 6,000 prisoners of war destined to meet the labor shortages on farms and with area businesses. The peak of 6,000 inmates under the Camp Perry umbrella coincided with the peak of 425,871 prisoners of war—371,683 Germans, 50,273 Italians and 3,915 Japanese—in 511 base camps and 175 branch camps throughout the United States in May 1945.[4] The prisoners of war were housed in hutments with military guards nearby to control any outbreaks of violence or negative actions toward fellow prisoners.[5]

Italian prisoners of war, after leaving Camp Perry, worked with civilians on ordnance at the adjacent Erie Proving Ground, including repairing 70 percent of the large guns used in the war effort. The proving ground employed more than five thousand people, including the prisoners of war. The civilians were housed in dormitories on-site and in government-provided prefabricated houses in a development called Erie Gardens in Port Clinton.

As the German prisoners of war continued to arrive, Camp Perry was the site of some resistance through work strikes and reaction to the newspaper *Der Ruf*, which was sent to the majority of base camps across the United States. Judith Gansberg reported that Nazi groups within the camps tried to prevent the distribution of *Der Ruf*, evidenced by signs posted at Camp Perry in March 1945 that read, when translated:

> *Do Americans believe they can force upon us a newspaper of traitors and deserters? All of you know by now Der Ruf! Shall we allow the Cologne and Trier to mock us? Do they want to tell us that we must regain our lost honor? Boycott! This shameful newspaper! Washington wants to "make an experiment" of us! (New York Times). But our honor means faith, our belief Germany! NOW MORE THAN EVER!"*[6]

Camp Perry's *Der Aufbau* newspapers released on October 6, December 8 and December 15, 1945, written by German prisoners of war just before their repatriation, reveal a contrary attitude to the March 1945 anti–*Der Ruf* signs, showing an evident distain for the Nazi regime and a subtle approval of the camp's re-education programs aimed at promoting the ideals and values of living in a democracy.

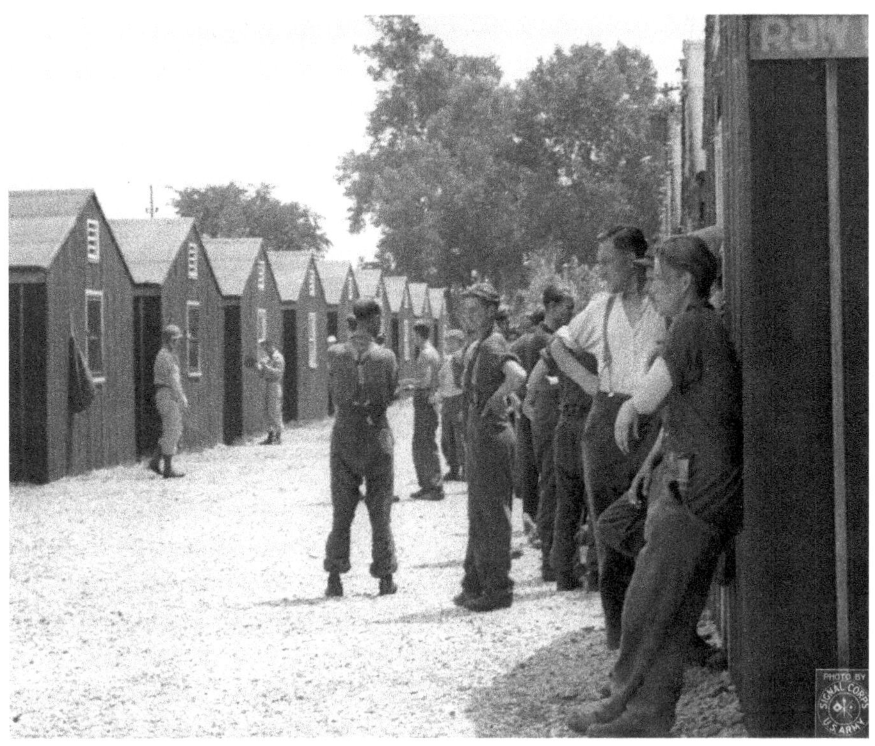

German prisoners of war outside of their hutments with American military guards nearby. *Courtesy of the Ottawa County Historical Museum, Peggy Debien, curator.*

Today, Camp Perry is an Ohio National Guard training facility and the largest outdoor rifle range in the world, host to the National Rifle Association–sponsored National Rifle Match and home to the Small Arms Firing School, which provides training and facilities for improving civilians' shooting skills.

1

THE NEW ARRIVALS

PRISONER OF WAR CAMPS IN THE UNITED STATES

The United States did not anticipate receiving thousands of prisoners of war that included Germans, Italians and Japanese. Had these prisoners of war consisted only of Italians and Japanese, the nation would have been able to handle this influx of prisoners, but with the additional Germans, the country strained to accommodate this huge number, as seen in the accompanying chart illustrating the timeframe of the prisoners' arrival. Peaking in June 1945, the total prisoner of war count of 425,606 consisted of 371,683 Germans, 50,273 Italians and 3,915 Japanese. In June 1946, there were 32,000 prisoners of war on military and civilian work projects, which terminated on June 15, 1946. All of the prisoners were repatriated by June 30, 1946, except 341 Germans, 29 Italians and 1 Japanese, who were serving sentences in U.S. penal institutions.[7]

The map shows the distribution of more than 600 base and branch prisoner of war camps in the United States during World War II. The proliferation proved to be a challenge for camp staff to maintain discipline and order within the camps from 1942 to 1946.[8]

The management of the prisoner of war camps was assigned to the Provost Marshal General Office, Prisoner of War Division, with the responsibility of providing resources to the camps.[9]

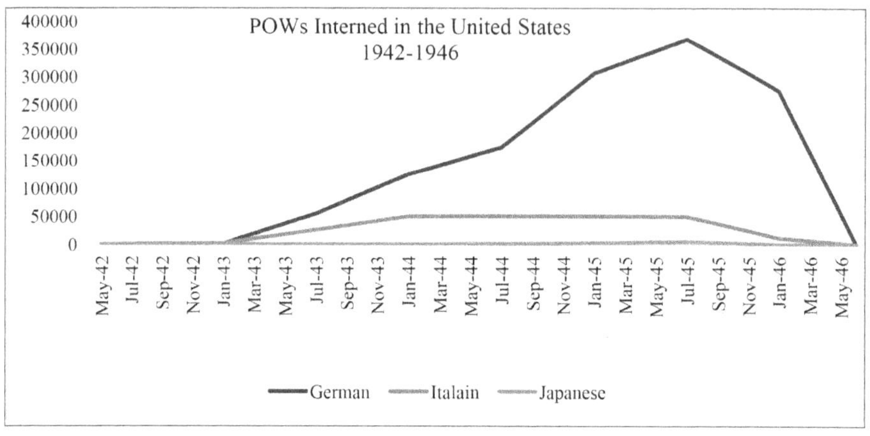

CHART 1. POWs Interned in the United States, 1942–1946. *Courtesy of Lewis and Mewba, 90–91.*

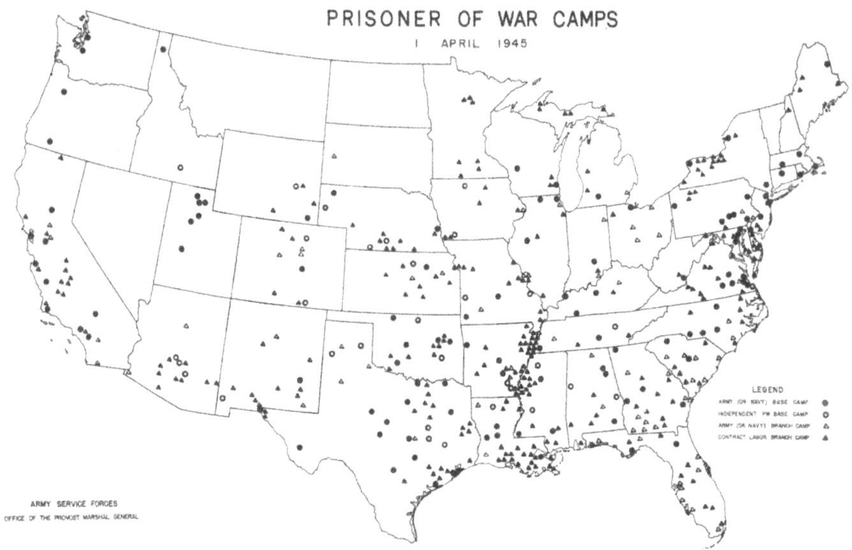

Map of prisoner of war base and branch camps across the United States, April 1, 1945. *Courtesy of NARA.*

The influx of prisoners of war to the United States started slowly in 1942, but by mid-August 1943 built up to a little more than 130,922, stemming from the successful North African campaign, which spurred an increase in the number of prisoners of war through June 1945. The Office of the Provost Marshal General directed that prisoners of war be

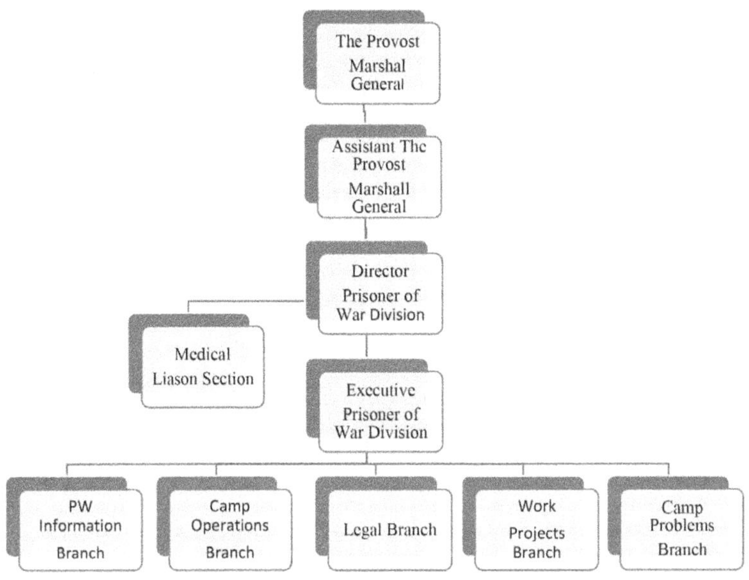

Chart 2. Provost Marshal General Office, Prisoner of War Division. *Courtesy of Lewis and Mewba, 121.*

segregated into different camps based on nationality and according to the following categories: (1) German army anti-Nazi prisoners; (2) remaining German army prisoners; (3) German navy anti-Nazi Germans; (4) remaining German navy prisoners; (5) Italian prisoners; and (6) Japanese prisoners. Prisoner of war officers were interned in the same camps but in different compounds from the enlisted prisoners.[10]

When prisoners of war reached the United States, they underwent a rigid interrogation and review process before they were sent to their permanent camps. The U.S. Army followed the guidelines of the Provost Marshal General Office as to where the prisoners of war were to be sent based on nationality, type of prisoner and camp. Once the German prisoners reached the United States, they were not only interrogated but also processed through a sequence of steps, as seen in the accompanying photographs showing an Iron Cross, Second Class, being removed from a prisoner's blouse[11] and German officers in line receiving their valuables.[12] The prisoners of war were allowed to retain their medals but not display them.

The Office of the Provost Marshal General had to scramble to find sites for prisoners of war camps, including such sites as military installations with

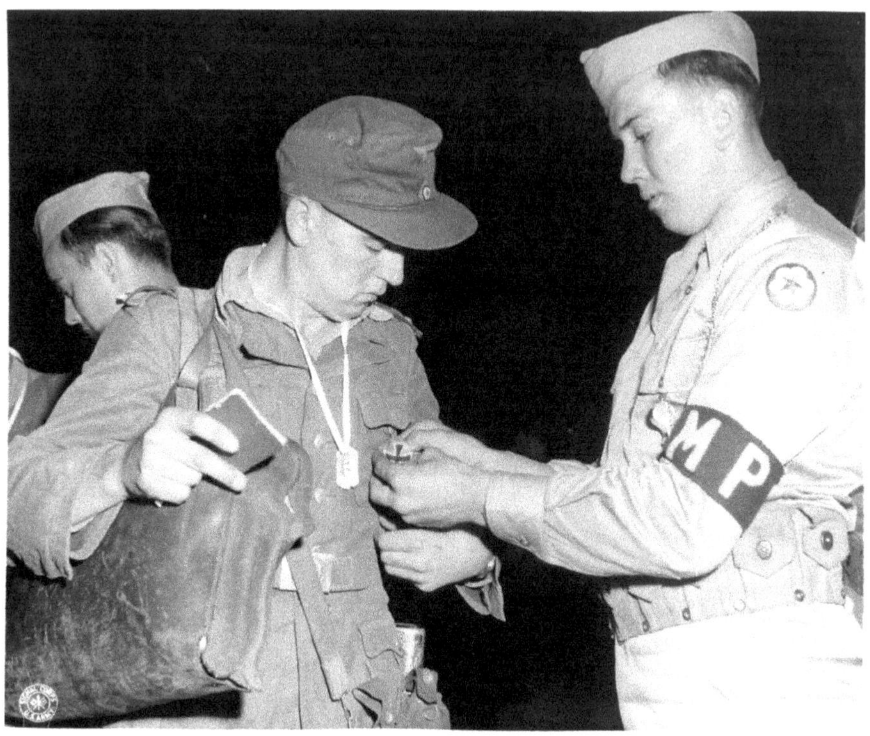

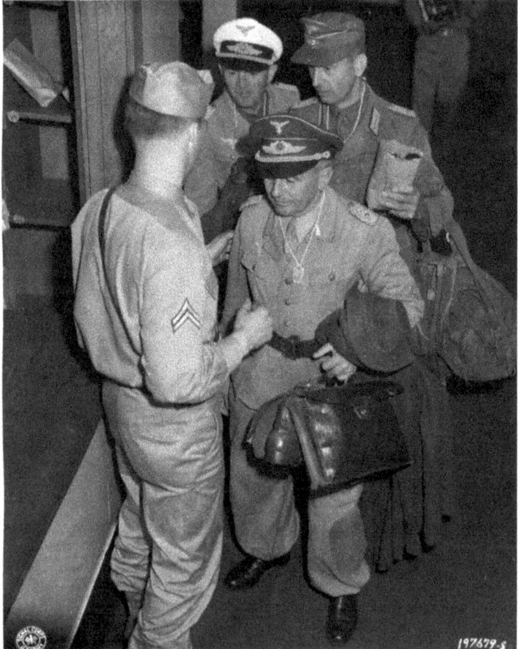

Above: Iron Cross, Second Class being removed from prisoners' blouses. *Courtesy of the NARA Photo No. SC 197669-s.*

Left: German POW officers waiting to receive valuables. *Courtesy of NARA Photo No. SC 197679-s.*

temporary housing that could later be converted into permanent housing. Once the prisoners of war camps were identified, the next problem was to develop a transportation system to disperse the prisoners of war across the United States. The photos show German prisoners of war having been processed at the port of Boston, Massachusetts, filing aboard a train with an armed guard atop the train[13] overlooking German officers and enlisted men headed to their permanent prisoner of war camps.[14]

The prisoner of war camps were organized similar to that shown in Typical Functional Chart: Base Prisoner of War Camp, where the camp commandment had the responsibility for coordinating the different areas listed in the chart. This oversight ensured that the base and branch camps fulfilled the articles of the Geneva Convention so that there would be no repercussions for mistreatment of prisoners of war.[15]

The Office of the Provost Marshal General, Prisoner of War Division, in conjunction with the Engineer Office of the South Atlantic Division,

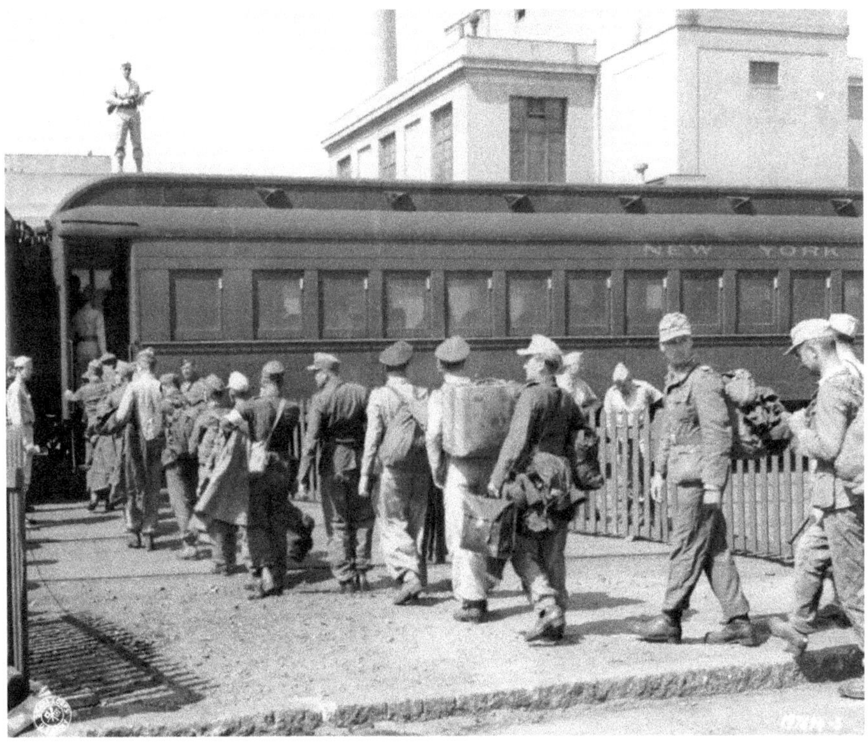

German POWs boarding a train. *Courtesy of NARA Photo No. SC 197674-s.*

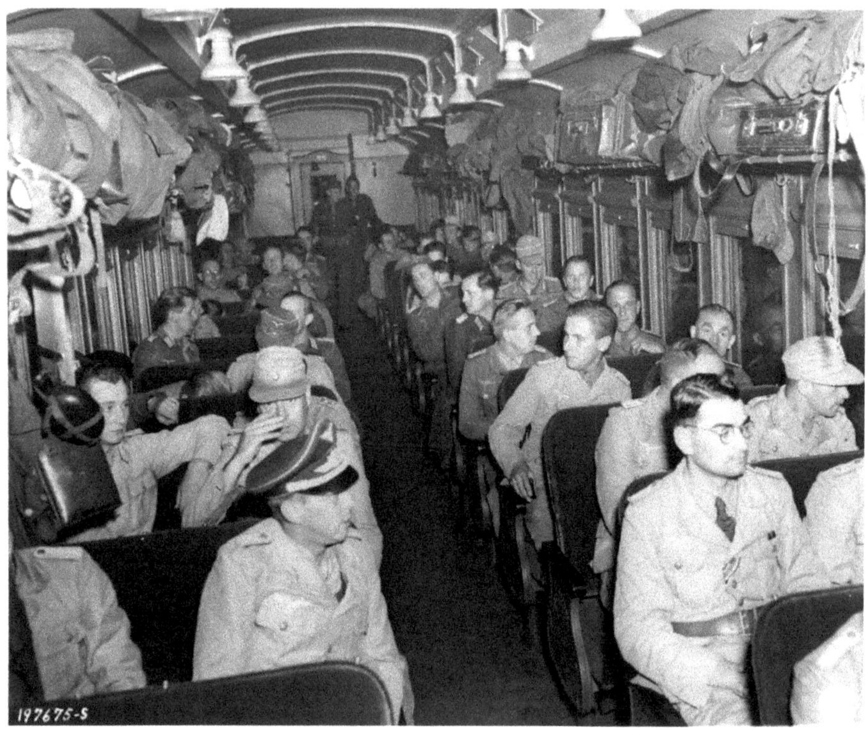

German POW officers aboard a train. *Courtesy of NARA Photo No. SC 197675-s.*

developed plans for proposing a 250-man-capacity tent and barracks prisoner of war labor camp, with the flexibility for future expansion. The camp layouts suggested requirements to conform to the Geneva Convention standards for providing adequate facilities for food, medical care and hygiene, and for sanitary conditions and recreation areas.[16]

Sports were important to the prisoners of war, especially those men who worked an eight-hour, five-day work schedule. The prisoners of war camps, pursuant to the Geneva Convention and the required layout plans, provided recreational fields for soccer teams and areas for chess and table tennis matches. The goal of many prisoners of war was to be the top team or individual in the camp and to see the scores and rankings posted in the camp newspaper.[17]

The layout plans illustrated fencing around the camps. The accompanying photo shows the main gate of a prisoner of war camp with two guards and two German POWs.[18]

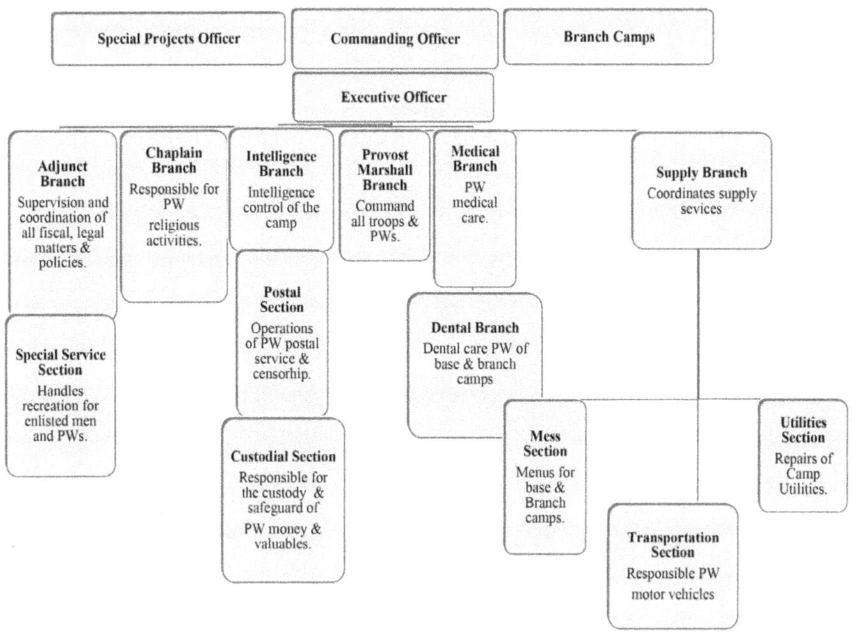

CHART 3. Typical Functional Chart: Base Prisoner of War Camp. *Courtesy of Lewis and Mewba, 149.*

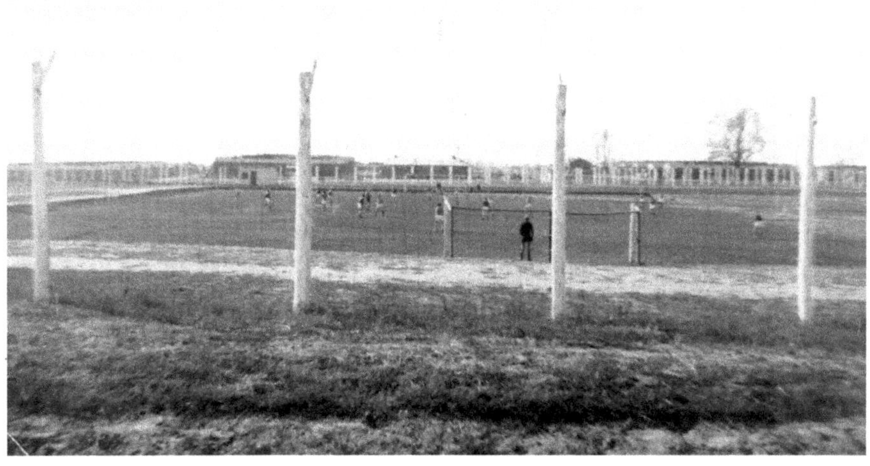

German athletic field. *Courtesy of the Ottawa County Historical Museum, Peggy Debien, curator.*

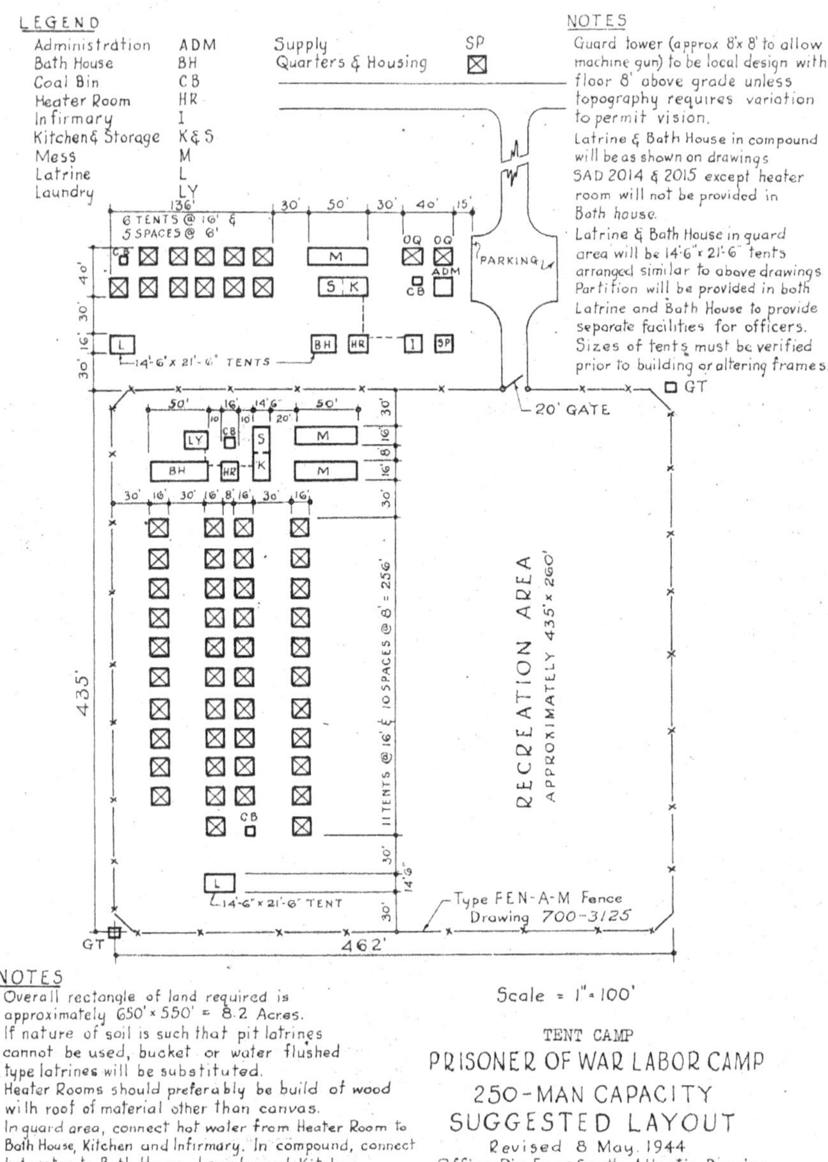

Prisoner of war labor camp tent layout. *Courtesy of NARA RG 389, 461: PMGO Inspection.*

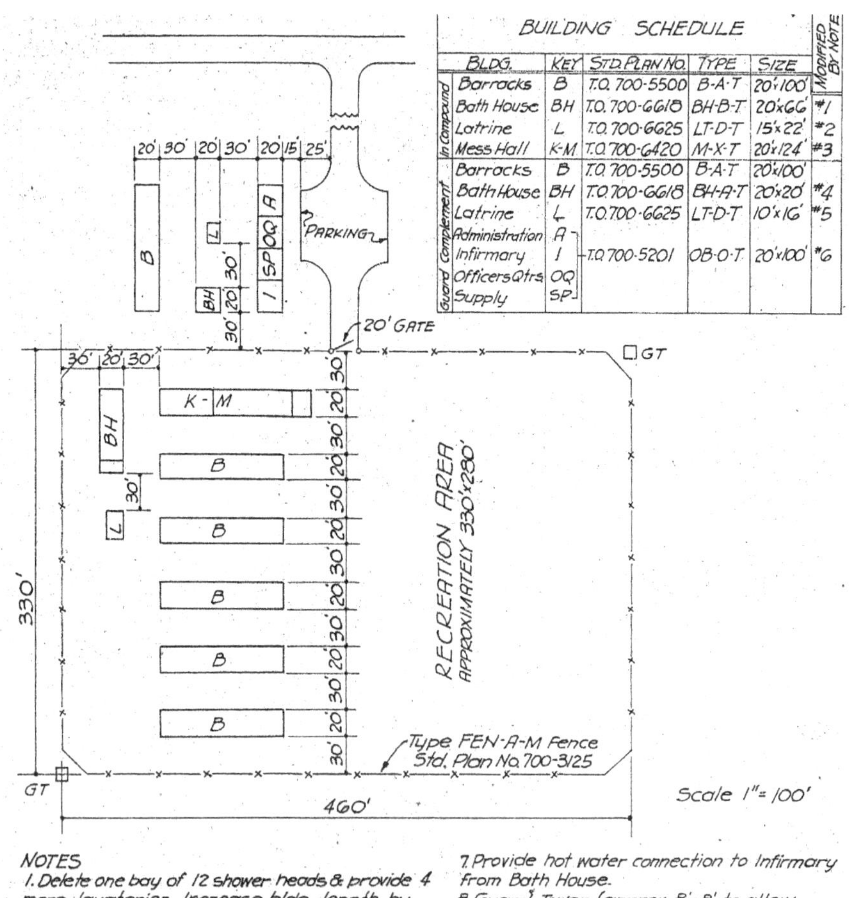

BUILDING SCHEDULE

	BLDG.	KEY	STD. PLAN NO.	TYPE	SIZE	MODIFIED BY NOTE
In Compound	Barracks	B	T.O. 700-5500	B-A-T	20'x100'	
	Bath House	BH	T.O. 700-6618	BH-B-T	20'x66'	#1
	Latrine	L	T.O. 700-6625	LT-D-T	15'x22'	#2
	Mess Hall	K-M	T.O. 700-6420	M-X-T	20'x124'	#3
Guard Complement	Barracks	B	T.O. 700-5500	B-A-T	20'x100'	
	Bath House	BH	T.O. 700-6618	BH-A-T	20'x20'	#4
	Latrine	L	T.O. 700-6625	LT-D-T	10'x16'	#5
	Administration	A				
	Infirmary	I	T.O. 700-5201	OB-O-T	20'x100'	#6
	Officers Qtrs	OQ				
	Supply	SP				

NOTES

1. Delete one bay of 12 shower heads & provide 4 more lavatories. Increase bldg. length by 10' and provide 10 laundry trays.
2. Increase length to 22', width to 15' and provide 16 holes in center, with 15' of urinal trough on each longitudinal sidewall.
3. Add 20'x 64' prisoner messing space and 20'x16' guard messing space to the 20'x 44' kitchen space.
4. Modify to provide 4 lav. for E.M. and partition to provide 1 lav. and 1 shower head in separate Officer space.
5. Modify to provide partition at mid-length with 4 holes and 5' of urinal trough. for E.M. and 1 hole and 3' of urinal trough for Officers.
6. Install 3 transverse partitions to provide 4 separate rooms.
7. Provide hot water connection to Infirmary from Bath House.
8. Guard Tower (approx. 8'x 8' to allow machine gun) to be of local design with floor 8' above grade unless topography requires elevation to permit vision.
9. Overall rectangle of land required is approximately 560'x560' = 7.2 acres.
10. If nature of soil is such that pit latrines can not be used, bucket or water flushed type latrines will be substituted.

PRISONER OF WAR LABOR CAMP
250 MAN CAPACITY
SUGGESTED LAYOUT
Office, Div. Engr. South Atlantic Division

Prisoner of war labor camp barracks layout, April 1, 1945. *Courtesy of NARA RG 389, 461: PMGO Inspection.*

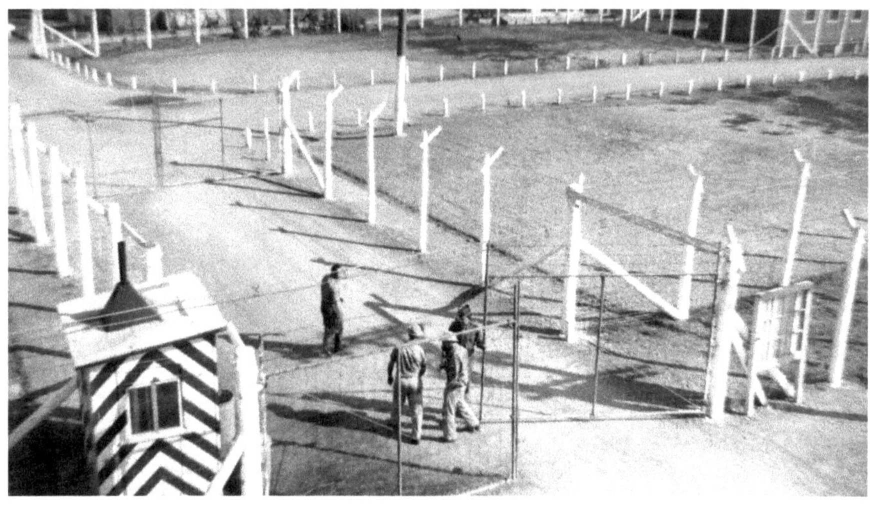

Main gate of a POW camp. *Courtesy of the Ottawa County Historical Museum, Peggy Debien, curator.*

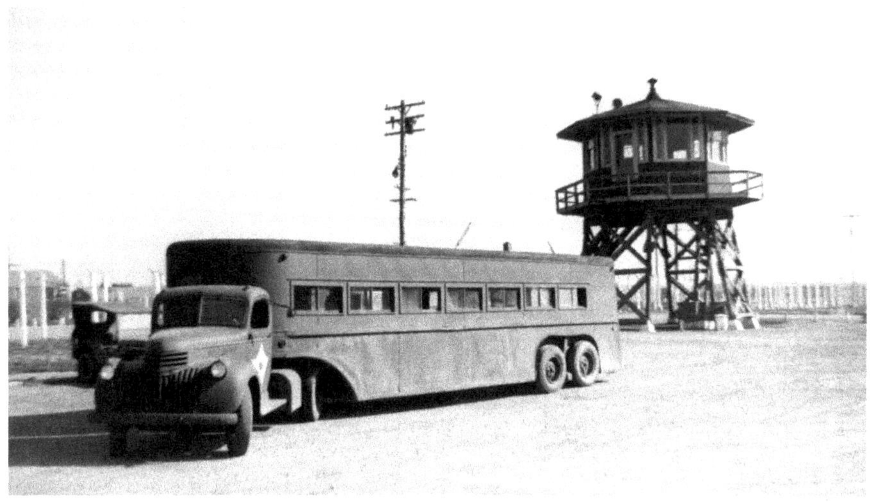

POW camp guard tower next to Bing Crosby's trailer. *Courtesy of the Ottawa County Historical Museum, Peggy Debien, curator.*

Also, the camp layout plans specified that the guard towers be eight feet by eight feet to allow for a machine gun, with the floor level being eight feet above grade or a height that allowed for clear vision of the fenced-in camp compound.[19]

INTERPRETERS AND SUPERVISION

One of the challenges for the Office of the Provost Marshal General was to hire interpreters for the base and branch camps and guards and civilian workers, especially when the prisoners of war were given contract work assignments outside the camps. It can be seen from the Typical Functional Chart: Base Prisoner of War Camp that this problem intensified in mid-August 1943, when schools were established to train prisoners in various trade areas before transferring them to camps to replace the civilian laborers who went off to war and left clerical and other vacancies at the camps.[20]

Many of the German and Italian prisoners of war were chosen as work supervisors because they spoke their native language and were asked to communicate with their fellow workers. But often, those called into this role, especially the Germans, were uncooperative and organized work stoppages and slowdowns that frequently led to violence and rebellion on the part of the prisoner laborers. "In some instances, threats of 'kangaroo courts,' violence, and family reprisals caused the PWs to fear these supervisors more than they respected the orders of the American PW camp commander." When these problems occurred, the camp commander would replace the prisoner of war supervisors with cooperative prisoners, regardless of rank. As the war progressed, it created a military manpower shortage; often, civilian supervisors were called on to oversee prisoner work projects. The accompanying chart is an example of the Disciplinary and Control Measures Applicable to Prisoners of War Form, which was used with prisoners of war who organized such activities as work stoppages and slowdowns.[21]

GUARDS

A major problem was finding qualified guards to maintain order in the camps. In the early part of the war, men selected as MPs were generally older, with an average age of early to mid-thirties; some were too old for service but did come to the job with a solid military background and experience. The goal was to maintain an adequate guard-to-prisoner ratio of one to three, but in reality, this became one to fifteen and placed a stress on the commanders at the prisoner of war camps to maintain order and

	Duration	Reprimand	Withholding Privileges	Guardhouse Restricted Limits	Hard Labor Without Pay
Administrative Pressure (all POWs)	Indefinite Until Compliance	Yes	Yes	Yes	No
Disciplinary 104th Article of War (all POWs)	7 days	Yes	Yes	Yes	EM-Yes NCOS Supv. only Offices–No
Summary Court-Martial (EM only)	30 days	Yes	Yes	Yes	Yes Including NCOS
Articles 54–59 Geneva Conv. (All POWs)	No	Yes	Yes	Yes	EM-Yes NCOS-Supervisory Only, Officers No
Judicial Suits —Special Court-Martial (EM) —General Court-Martial (All POWs)	As provided by the Articles of War, Army Regulations, Geneva Convention, Manual of Court-Martial. Note: The Geneva Convention requires notice be given to protecting power in all judicial suits, notice transmitted through PMGO, notice must be given more than three weeks prior to trial. Also of action of reviewing authority and of confirming authority. Other pertinent requirements: Choice of defense counsel and competent interpreter furnished to prisoner.				

Responsibility for Impositions	Camp Commander	Company Commander	Company Commander	No
Use of Physical Force	No	No	No	No
Forfeiture pay & Allowances	Discontinue of $2 allow. EM only-prorate	No	Yes	$2 EM Monthly Allowance
Withholding Pay & Allowances	Yes (Pay/ allowance)	Yes	Yes	Yes all Pay/ Allow.
Restricted Diet	Yes	No	No	14 days only

NO POW MAY BE REDUCED IN RANK OR GRADE, BY COURT-MARTIAL OR OTHERWISE

Chart 4. Disciplinary and Control Measures Applicable to Prisoners of War Form. *Courtesy of Lewis and Mewba, 154.*

prevent prisoner revolts.[22] The need for all able-bodied soldiers to be on the front lines as the war progressed necessitated the following memo of March 24, 1944, sent to camp commanders:

> *Because huge numbers of German prisoners are expected in the immediate future, camp administrators are advised to let prisoners do everything in the running the camps. Weigh work done against Reasoner risk. In other words, take a calculated risk. This policy of calculated risk will result in larger reductions of American guard personnel, the majority of whom can be transferred to combat units for action in France.*[23]

Even with this memo, which gave the German prisoners of war authority to run a portion of the camps, it created a situation in which committed Nazis could control their fellow prisoners with threats of violence, a censorship program to review incoming and outgoing mail and the operation of newspapers that removed any articles unfavorable to Germany. Portraits of Hitler were also found throughout the camps, promoted by the committed Nazis.

According to Arnold Krammer's paper "German Prisoners of War in the United States," even though the War Department knew that some Nazis controlled prisoner of war camps, the War Problems Division released a memo in August 1944 allowing for the reintroduction of the Nazi salute as an accepted greeting at prisoner of war camps. The memo stated:

> *The new salute has, of course, distinct Nazi implications but so have the Swastika on German uniforms and decorations which the prisoners of war are allowed to display. We might be able to gain some advantages: personnel can endeavor to keep careful track of the prisoners who seem to be enthusiastic about the Nazi salute. A count of Nazi noses could thus become possible. The Nazi salute should not be made fun of or commented on by American guard personnel within hearing of the prisoners of war. The best way of treating it would seem to be the old fashion American poker-faced method. In the course of time many prisoners will tend to get tired of it.*[24]

This kind of action by the War Problems Division reinforced the principles of Nazism for those prisoners of war who believed Germany would win the war. The use of the salute was also a way for hardcore Nazis to identify those prisoners who had turned anti-Nazi and then discipline them, which often led to violence within the camps and created control issues for the camp commandants.

A survey of German prisoners of war in Europe in 1944 found the following: (1) 100 percent had confidence in Hitler, (2) 56 percent believed that Germany would win, (3) 55 percent had a preference for National Socialism after the war, (4) 28 percent had an uncompromising unwillingness to accept defeat, (5) 25 percent held that Hitler's government would continue to lose the war, and (6) 10 percent believed that a soldier must under all circumstances obey orders to fight to the last bullet.[25] One can see from this survey that camp commanders often faced Nazi prisoners who still had faith in Hitler, believed that Germany would win the war and held an unwillingness to accept defeat, beliefs that led to efforts by this group to be controlling and disruptive in the camps.

PRISONER OF WAR LABOR SUPERVISORS

In the *Handbook for Work Supervisors of Prisoner of War Labor* (July 1945), supervisors were reminded that the men they were overseeing were not criminals and that they followed their leaders for the national cause, good or bad. It must be remembered that the German prisoners of war were patriotic and had made great sacrifices for their country, and because of this the supervisors were instructed not to argue with, use abusive language toward or make disparaging remarks about Germany in the presence of the prisoners. The supervisors were also instructed not to refer to the prisoners of war as "Krauts" or "Heinies" in their presence. They were taught to be stoic and to not attempt to punish or reprimand the prisoners of war, a task that was left up to the camp commander.[26]

The supervisors were to set examples for the prisoners of war by being neat in appearance as a means of instilling respect for their supervision in the workplace. They were trained to be aware of the Germans' belief that Americans were bad managers and that Germans were the superior race. Because of these feelings, the supervisors had to show the prisoners that they were misguided in their assessment of the American worker while at the same time holding on to their role as tough taskmasters.[27]

The supervisors pushed the prisoners of war to fulfill their quotas so that they would be granted leisure time to pursue hobbies and recreational activities. The Germans were fanatic about exercise as a means of staying physically fit, even though they were confined to a stockade surrounded by a barbed-wire fence and guard towers.

Since the U.S. newspapers often carried stories about the prisoners of war being coddled, the supervisors were instructed not to pander to the prisoners, as this would antagonize the public and create more negative publicity, especially if it was perceived that the prisoners were replacing civilians in the workplace. As a result, the supervisors had to first make sure that qualified civilians were not available for the work assigned to the prisoners.

The supervisors were instructed that the workplace must be a safe environment and that the prisoners of war should not handle high-speed cutting tools nor climb to dangerous heights. German officers and those of equivalent rank were not forced to work, but permission to work could be granted by the camp commander. The supervisors were told not to use noncommissioned officers in a supervisory capacity, since it was believed that they did not make good supervisors. The prisoners of war were entitled to twenty-four hours of rest one day a week, which was to be approved by the camp commander and usually occurred on Sundays. If prisoners of war refused to work, the camp commander, not the supervisor, could take away privileges from the prisoners of war. Supervisors were instructed that rest periods were not mandatory, and if they were to be granted, they should be given in the morning or afternoon; however, the first priority was to get the work done and drive to the finish line.[28]

The overall plan for supervising the German prisoners of war was to maximize production, and this was achieved by the supervisors using the following approaches: (1) remembering the prisoners' background; (2) knowing the rights of both supervisors and prisoners of war; (3) taking into consideration prisoner aptitudes, qualifications and characteristics; (4) determining the best use for each individual; and (5) treating prisoners impersonally and requiring civilians on the job to do the same. Another key element in supervising the workforce was that the supervisors were instructed not to work the men in teams when their personalities did not mesh while at the same time looking for unique abilities, such as technical and professional skills, that could be leveraged in the workplace.[29]

It is evident that the supervisors had to be diplomats impervious to criticism and the recalcitrant attitudes of some of the German prisoners of war. The supervisors found that by following the guidelines developed by the Army Services Forces they were able to obtain maximum production from the labor pool and consistently achieve a full day's work from the prisoners of war.

WORK PROGRAMS

The work program became an integral part of the prisoner of war camps to make up for the lack of manpower in the United States caused by the large number of men serving in the armed services. Before the prisoners of war became a part of the U.S. workforce, there needed to be training in all trades, and before the training could begin there needed to be enough interpreters to assist with the training. This often meant that those prisoners of war who were identified as cooperative were asked to be the link between trainer and trainee. Private contractors employed most of the prisoners of war. These contractors were taking a chance with a prisoner of war who might cause hostilities in the workplace that could lead to sabotage or even violence against other employees and the employer. In many cases, labor unions objected to the prisoners in the workplace, claiming they were displacing qualified American workers; sometimes this only exasperated the situation, especially in work areas where there was a strong union presence.

The pay rates for prisoners of war were as follows:

> *1. Enlisted prisoners of war received a $3.00 stipend of canteen coupons or savings, whether they worked or not.*
> *2. Enlisted prisoners of war who worked received $.80 per day, which was later increased to $1.20 per day.*
> *3. Noncommissioned officers, depending on rank, were paid $5.00–$10.00 per month, depending on rank.*
> *4. Noncommissioned officers were not required to work but worked as supervisors to receive additional pay.*
> *5. Commissioned officers, in accordance with the Geneva Convention, did not have to work and received $20–$40 per month depending on rank.*[30]

As a means of placating the unions and giving some guidance to private contractors, the War Department issued to its field personnel on August 14, 1943, the following instructions for hiring prisoners of war:

> *A. Prisoners of war will be employed only when labor is available and cannot be recruited from other areas within a reasonable length of time.*
> *B. Before the War Manpower Commission certifies to the need for using prisoners of war, all supplies of labor, including secondary sources, within the area from which workers normally come to perform work of this type must be exhausted.*

> *C. Prisoners of War shall not be used in any way which will impair the wages, working conditions, and employment conditions of resident labor.*
> *D. As evidence of the fact the use of prisoners of war will not affect local conditions of employment adversely, the employer must place a bona fide order for workers needed with the local employment office. It is advisable to allow the local office a reasonable time to fill the order before preparing a certificate of the need for prisoners of war. This order must meet the following conditions:*
> *1. Contain no discriminatory specifications.*
> *2. Wage rates must not be less than the rate prevailing in the locality for similar work.*
> *3. Working conditions must be equivalent to those prevailing in the Locality for civilian workers performing similar jobs.*[31]

The Geneva Convention specified that prisoners of war were not permitted to perform war-related work, but because of a labor shortage in 1944, this rule was reinterpreted to allow for work in army equipment rebuilding, machine shops and factory work that contributed to the war effort but was unconnected to munitions and the like. In 1945, the War Department again loosened restrictions for prisoners of war working on military installations by creating an exhaustive list of work options unrelated to the war that could be done at military installations. During the time the prisoners were in the United States, their labor responsibilities were designated by the following categories: (1) Priority I essential work for maintenance and operation of military installations, (2) Priority II contact labor with private employers and (3) useful but nonessential work on or connected with military installations.[32]

The demand for prisoner of war work continued to increase, and by April 1945, the percentage of prisoners of war working reached 91.3 percent and eventually to a level where the demand exceeded the number of available prisoners at the end of war in Europe. The number of man-months from June 1944 to August 1945 totaled 851,994, broken out across the industries listed in the accompanying chart.[33]

Agriculture	439,163
Plywood, lumber	165,743
Mining, quarrying	2,738
Construction	9,940
Food processing	110,789
Other manufacturing	46,840

Transportation	1,469
Trade	8,558
Other nongovernment work	11,823
Public	50,931

Chart 5. Man-Months, June 1944–August 1945. *Courtesy of Lewis and Mewba, 121.*

With VE Day, prisoners of war started to be shipped back home, which meant there would be a gap in man-months. There was concern as to how the nation would fill the labor gap, with more than 400,000 deaths and 1 million wounded or seriously wounded soldiers returning home. Most of the concern came from farmers, who were losing cheap labor and did not know how many local men would return home able to work.

RE-EDUCATING PRISONERS OF WAR

Article 17 of the Geneva Convention stated that the belligerent country could provide for intellectual pursuits by prisoners of war. The U.S. State Department examined the interpretation of the article and initially worked through the Swiss government to connect with the Reich Minister for Science, Art, and Education to develop classes that could lead to degrees in Germany. Prisoners of war could earn high school equivalency diplomas, take elementary and secondary education courses and exams, in addition to earning other professional training degrees as designated by the German government. American prisoners of war in Germany had a similar arrangement for course and degree opportunities transferable to the United States.[34] In both cases, the courses were taught by qualified Americans or German prisoners of war, the latter paid based on a scale established at camp. The photo of German prisoners of war attending an evening class in draftsmanship[35] is illustrative of Germans going through a re-education program in which they were given an opportunity to go to school with the aim that the education programs would prepare them for better lives after the war. Many took mathematics, language, science and other subjects while in the camps.

As more prisoners of war came to the United States, a more propaganda-focused re-education program started to take place at the camps that likely violated the Geneva Convention's protocol forbidding prisoners of war

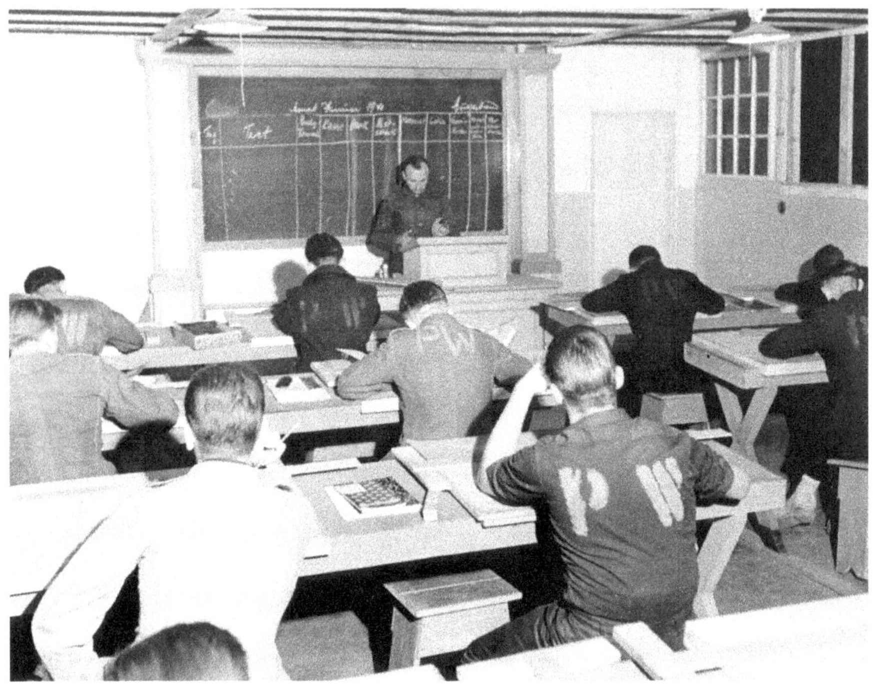

German prisoners of war attending an evening class in draftsmanship. *Courtesy of NARA Photo: 208-AA-309Z-2.*

from being propagandized through education. The Prisoner of War Special Project Division developed a program called "Intellectual Diversion" with classes pushing democratic ideals. Values started to take shape across camps, and a film branch was established that presented American movies aimed at subtly portraying the benefits of the American way of life over National Socialism.

In 1945, the newspaper *Der Ruf* ("The Call") was introduced to try to instill democratic ideals in the German prisoners of war so that when they were repatriated they would consider establishing a more democratic kind of government in Germany versus the continuation of the National Socialism approach. The newspaper told of the progress of the war, news from Germany—especially as the country began to lose the war—and, of course, the good things in American culture.

Selected prisoners worked in special camps as translators and counselors who developed guidelines for broad re-education and democratization programs in the prisoner of war camps across the United States. Additional responsibilities for developing and promoting these programs were given to prisoners to edit newspapers at the camps, review films for the camps and translate pamphlets for distribution in the camps. It should be noted that these volunteers were often accused of being turncoats, especially by the more hostile German prisoners of war.

ITALIAN SERVICE UNITS (ISUS)

In the fall of 1943, Italy became a co-belligerent, as seen in the accompanying photo,[36] which placed the Italian prisoners of war in a unique situation, since Italy was now assisting the United States with its war effort against Germany and Japan. At first, an Italian prisoner of war parole system was developed that allowed the prisoners to work without guards, even outside of the camps. These prisoners later moved on to join the Italian Service Unit (ISU), where they became volunteers. There they were given a khaki or medium-blue uniform consisting of a green cotton shirt, trousers and a cap.[37] A green patch of Italy adorned the left sleeve of the shirt and oftentimes the cap as well. Table 1, Deployment of Italian Service Units, June 30, 1944, and June 30, 1945,[38] illustrates the organizational structure of Italian Service Units in the United States, which accounted for approximately 64 percent of the Italians housed in prisoner of war camps.

Recruited ISU members were to assist with the labor shortage in the United States, with the first employment being in the agricultural sector. Recruitment of Italian soldiers was bolstered through such incentives as receiving twenty-four dollars per month, with eight dollars in cash and sixteen dollars in canteen coupons, or a trust fund that could be used to buy anything on or off the camp. ISU officers were paid twenty-four dollars on top of their monthly stipend. The recruitment was so successful that ISU members represented approximately 65 percent of the Italian prisoners of war.[39]

Historic Context: World War II Prisoner-of-War Camps on Department of Defense Installations provides a snapshot of the level of freedom experienced by ISU members:

> *These men selected for ISU were "free" like soldiers in the American Army. They still had restrictions placed upon them to safeguard themselves, the Army, and any civilians they might come in contact with during the performance of their duties. It was also important to the Army, from a*

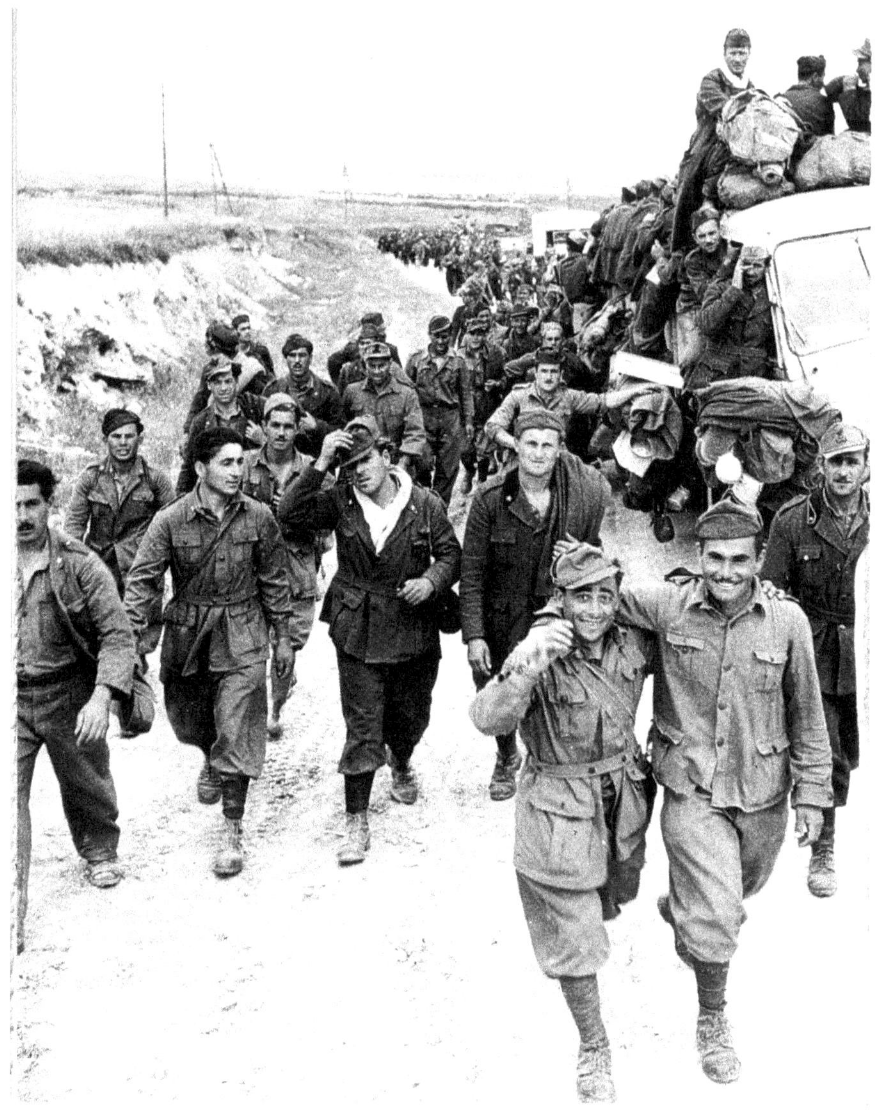

Italian prisoners of war in Tunisia before coming to the United States. *Courtesy of the Ottawa Historical Museum, Peggy Debien, curator.*

public relations standpoint, that these units be greeted with acceptance by the American people. Since some of these former prisoners would indeed be working with little or no Army supervision off-post, only those thought to be the most trustworthy were assigned to units allowing them almost total freedom of movement.[40]

*Table 3. Deployment of Italian Service Units, 30 June 1944 and 30 June 1945**

Status	Number of units	Strength	
		Officers	Enlisted men
30 June 1944			
Total	183	1, 041	33, 828
On duty:			
Headquarters, Fort Wadsworth, N. Y.	1	50	53
Service Command installations	25	144	4, 040
1st	0	0	0
2d	3	12	447
3d	3	12	645
4th	2	10	321
5th	5	21	486
6th	0	0	0
7th	0	0	0
8th	1	4	116
9th	11	85	2, 025
Technical Service installations	110	540	19, 205
Transportation Corps	56	259	9, 503
Ordnance	31	134	5, 724
Quartermaster	19	132	3, 359
Signal Corps	3	13	452
Engineer	0	0	0
Provost Marshal General	1	2	167
Air Force installations	0	0	0
In training	47	307	10, 530
31 July 1945			
Total	195	1, 116	31, 333
On duty:			
Headquarters, Fort Wadsworth, N. Y.	1	37	49
Service Command installations	35	150	4, 603
1st	0	0	0
2d	6	26	741
3d	1	6	193
4th	4	22	529
5th	7	34	710
6th	1	3	107
7th	0	0	0
8th	1	5	201
9th	15	54	2, 122
Technical Service installations	158	925	26, 496
Transportation Corps	70	279	11, 106
Ordnance	49	237	8, 549
Quartermaster	24	124	4, 057
Signal Corps	4	14	634
Engineer	10	98	1, 988
Provost Marshal General	1	[a] 175	162
Air Force installations	1	4	185
In training	0	0	0

* *Source:* WD, ASF Monthly Progress Reports, sec. 11, 31 Jul 44 and 31 Jul 45.
[a] Members of Enemy Section, Prisoner of War Information Bureau, Fort George G. Meade, Md.

TABLE 1. Deployment of Italian Service Unit (ISU). *Courtesy of Lewis and Mewba, 96.*

Prisoners of war who did not join the ISU missed out on receiving the eighty cents per day in scrip for labor beyond housekeeping responsibilities and ten cents for necessities. Non-ISU members were also not allowed to participate in social activities outside the camp free from military oversight, as ISU members were. Eventually, ISU members would in some cases leave their agriculture work and go to work on military bases or in some cases be allowed to work in war-related industries other than munitions. ISU members played a key role in picking up the labor shortage in the United States across most labor industries except the munitions sector, as those positions were unavailable to German prisoners of war. Unlike German prisoners of war, ISU members could socialize outside the camps at local gatherings and even attend sporting events. The data in the accompanying chart illustrates the number of man-days of ISU programs as of March 31, 1944, days that relieved U.S. service personnel for their overseas duty.[41]

• Transportation Corps for overseas distribution	2,000,000
• Ordnance Corps depots and arsenals	1,364,374
• Quartermaster Corps preparing supplies	800,000
• Engineer Corps	333,000
• Military installations reconditioning vehicles	750,000
• Total Man-Days	5,247,374

CHART 6. Man-Days, ISU Program, March 31, 1944. *Courtesy of Lewis and Mewba, 100.*

OBSERVATIONS

The arrival of the prisoners of war created major logistical problems for the Office of the Provost Marshal General, which was assigned the responsibility for running the camps. They had to find camp locations across the county, train guards and interpreters, develop interrogation and relocation processes and, eventually, create re-education programs aimed at instilling democratic ideals in the minds of the prisoners of war. One of the camp commandant's major challenges were the hardcore Nazi prisoners of war, who still believed that Germany was going to win the war and carried forth that attitude to the camps. They intimidated anti-Nazi prisoners through harassment and physical abuse. The Italian Service Unit members, because their county had become a co-belligerent, did not present the same challenges as the German prisoners of war and were thus given work assignments at the Erie Proving Ground and the Marion and Rossford ordnance depots. The logistics and preparation done by the Office of the Provost Marshal General developed on-the-fly guidelines that made it possible for Camp Perry and its branch camps to function as well-organized, cohesive units.

2

PRISONER OF WAR ARRIVALS AT CAMP PERRY

Camp Perry, like other prisoner of war camps in the United States, was established to alleviate the overcrowding prisoner of war camps in Great Britain. The camp was built on flat land, part of the Lake Erie Coastal Plain, with the military reservation on about 760 acres and the prisoner of war camp occupying approximately 32 acres that, before its closing in 1946, allowed for the capacity to house 3,000 men. Each of the 5-man, single-story, sixteen-foot-by-sixteen-foot tar-paper-covered hutments consisted of a wood-framed building on concrete slabs and double-paned windows, with heat provided by a central wood-burning stove vented through the roof. The hutments were evenly spaced in rows of twelve, with a set of four bathhouses for nine rows, providing services for 108 hutments and 545 men. A nine-strand barbed-wire fence nine feet high surrounded the stockade with eleven guard towers spaced around the fenced-in stockade. The mess halls and latrines were constructed of concrete blocks with concrete floors. The hospital wards had a capacity of 105 beds and were located near the station hospital at Camp Perry, about two miles away.[42]

Camp Perry was the largest prisoner of war camp in Ohio and accorded the prisoners many privileges of an educational and recreational nature. The thrust of the educational programs at Camp Perry was to teach English to prisoners of war so that they could read American magazines and books provided by the library. American history was also taught at the camp, not as history but as a vehicle for the prisoners to gain a better understanding of the American way of life and democratic values. The camp provided excellent recreational amenities for the prisoners, including a large athletic field, movie theaters and other artistic outlets, as well as a recreation hall for card playing and other games. There was even a canteen and beer garden that allowed the prisoners of war to relax after a long, hard day of work in the fields or local industries.

Camp Perry made an effort to provide religious opportunities for the prisoners of war, as evidenced when the Italians converted a building into a church and a location for the Germans in 1943 for their church services. In both cases, the camp commandant, Lieutenant Colonel E.C. McCormick Jr., made every attempt to provide Italian- and German-speaking priests and ministers for church services and other religious gatherings.

Lieutenant Colonel E.C. McCormick Jr., who before the war ended rose from major to colonel on account of his leadership and organizational skills, was camp commander of Camp Perry and its branch camps, which meant overseeing more than six thousand prisoners of war. The base camp officers in charge with multiple duties when the camp opened are shown in the accompanying chart.[43]

Rank	Name	Duties
Major	E.C. McCormick Jr.	Camp Commander
2nd Lt.	Robert D. Putvin	Adjutant (Principal Duty)
		Fiscal Officer
		Personnel Officer (Additional Duties)
		Postal Officer
		Insurance/Bond Officer
1st Lt.	Julius N. Valentinelli	Chaplain (Principal Duty)
1st Lt.	Frank Bodenhorn	Operations Officer (Principal Duty)
		Contract Officer
		Work Amts Officer
		Public Relations Officer (Additional Duties)
		Visitors Officer
		Commanding Officer, Headquarters Detachment
2nd Lt.	Yale Fish	Supply Officer (Principal Duty)
		Bakery Officer
		Tailor Shop Officer (Additional Duties)
		Tool Officer

RANK	NAME	DUTIES
2nd Lt.	Alvan E. Estep	Commanding Officer, Co. "B" (Principal Duty) Special Service Officer Canteen Officer (Additional Duties) Barber Shop Officer
2nd Lt.	Orville E. Lewis	Commanding Officer, Co. "D" (Principal Duty) Theater Officer (Additional Duty)
2nd Lt.	Benjamin L. Kiesling	Commanding Officer, Co. "C" (Principal Duty) Cobbler Shop Officer (Additional Duty)
Captain	Henry Collins	Prison Officer (Principal Duty) Commanding Officer, Co. "A" (Additional Duties) Complaints Officer

CHART 7. Base Camp Officers Duties. *Courtesy of NARA, PMGO Inspection Reports, 1943.*

ARRIVAL OF ITALIAN PRISONERS OF WAR

The War Department announced in the October 1, 1943 edition of the *Port Clinton Herald and Republican* that Camp Perry would receive a limited number of Italian prisoners of war, with the aim of having them do some work on the military reservations as well as contract work off the base. Given the shortage of manpower in the tomato fields and fruit orchards, this influx of Italian prisoners would assist in filling the local labor gap. Some residents expressed concerns about having a prisoner of war camp in their backyards, while others, according to the newspaper, stated: "This is war and we'll have to make the best of it."[44]

The Italian prisoners of war were given the opportunity to sign an agreement obligating them to change their allegiance to the American pursuit of the German army. Those who signed the agreement became members of the Italian Service Unit (ISU). In the beginning, there were four companies of prisoners of war, each company consisting of an American first sergeant, American supply sergeant, American company clerk and an Italian Master Maresciallo (warrant officer), who was the highest-ranking noncommissioned officer in the Italian army and in charge of each company and each platoon. The interpreters were prisoners of war who spoke English.

The October 16, 1943 edition of the *Port Clinton Herald and Republican* featured the headline: "Gracia Americans! Italian Prisoners Happy at Camp Perry: Have Own Mascot." The article began, "If I'm any judge of facial expressions, the several hundred Italians prisoners of war, quartered at Camp Perry are as happy a group of individuals you'll find anywhere behind barbed wire."[45] The initial group of prisoners of war did salvage work at the Erie Proving Ground. Their mascot was a mongrel dog captured along with them by the American troops. The prisoners of war were not required to work, but some elected to do groundskeeping work and the repairing of their buildings. Each company had its own mess hall next to the hutments where the prisoners of war prepared their own food, work that included cleaning salmon, chopping onions, mixing highly flavored tomato sauce, cooking string beans, and preparing what resembled and tasted like American stew. A specialty of the Italians was "coffee soup," a mixture of coffee, milk, cream and bread that formed a soupy substance relished by the prisoners of war.[46] Another Italian specialty, of course, was spaghetti. These men were also assigned to the mess halls to serve the meals.[47]

Camp commander McCormick was well liked by the prisoners because he treated them fairly during their internment. The October 16, 1943 *Port Clinton Herald and Republican* stated: "And one can see from his preliminary work that when the International Red Cross inspects the camp and makes its report to both the Italian and German governments, another 'good mark' will be recorded in the record books of American History."[48] This same article pointed out that the Italians took part in all the activities available to them and spent hours brushing their teeth so that they gleamed like pearls.

The Italian prisoners of war were organized into Quartermaster and Engineer Battalion units. Those who volunteered to serve in ISUs were organized in a military fashion, despite the fact they would not serve in combat. They were awarded special privileges and liberties they had not received as prisoners of war, in accordance with the Italians' co-belligerent efforts. ISUs were staffed with Italian officers and noncommissioned officers. Its members wore distinctive uniforms featuring the word "ITALY"

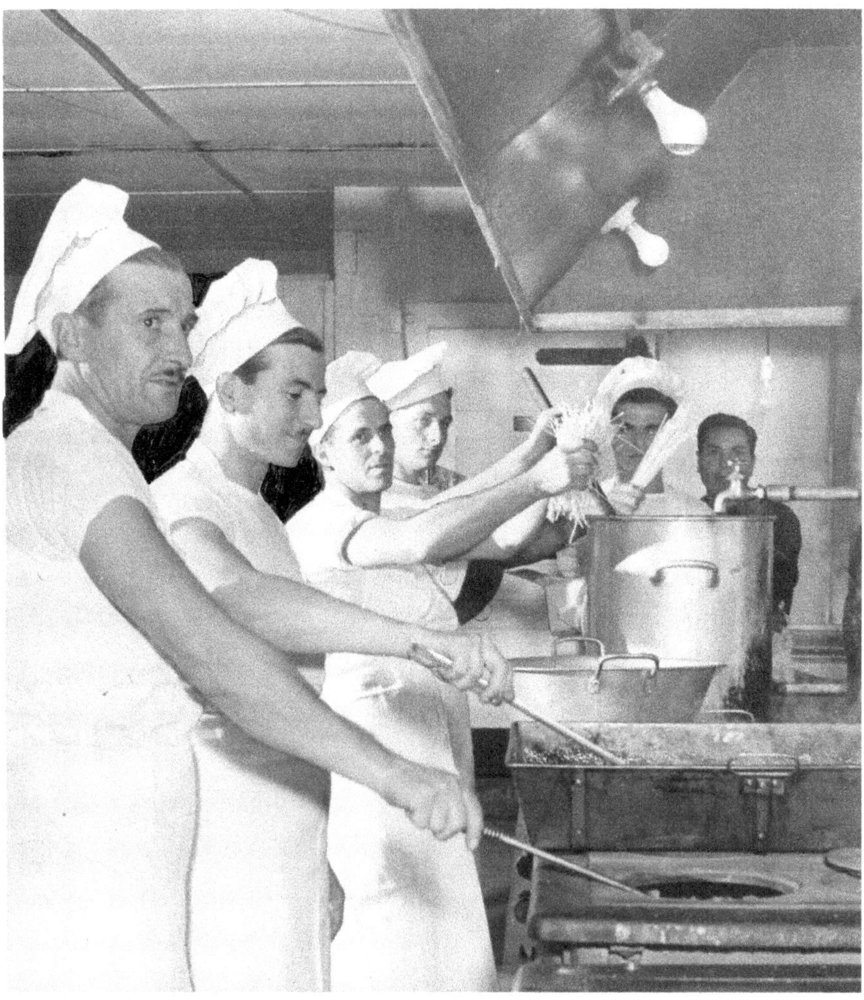

Italian prisoners of war cooking spaghetti in a kitchen at Camp Perry. *Courtesy of the Ottawa County Historical Museum, Peggy Debien, curator.*

emblazoned in white block letters both on the left sleeves of their green brassards and in the red and green patches of their caps. On the back of each uniform were the orange letters *PW*, the designation for prisoner of war. Those accepted into the ISU had to be mentally and physically qualified, clear military intelligence and sign an application for assignment that promised to serve out any task, except combat, that would aid in the war effort against Germany. Privileges were revoked for any disciplinary infraction.[49] Even though ISU members did not see combat, they nonetheless

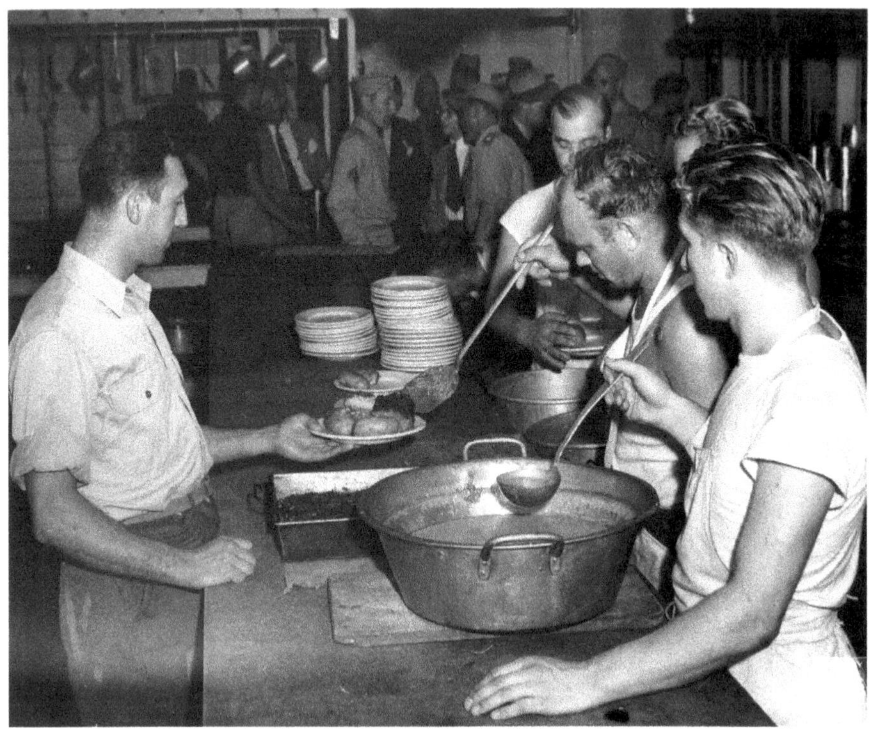

Italian prisoners of war serving food in a mess hall at Camp Perry. *Courtesy of the Ottawa County Historical Museum, Peggy Debien, curator.*

went through routine marching exercises that included close-order drills and marches with backpacks, all part of the ISU training.[50]

The American public was reassured that the Quartermaster Battalion would not replace civilian workers but would instead assist in shops and farms where labor support was needed. The Italians went through on-the-job training on the base that prepared them for their future work. ISU members continued to be paid their present rate, with a portion of their earnings in cash and the remainder in post-exchange coupons or, alternatively, with the entire sum paid in coupons.[51]

Colonel F.E. Rondell, stationed at the Erie Proving Ground, stated: "Those men that have signed up for this limited service apparently are inspired by a sincere desire to assist in the defeat of our enemies. It is believed that as their training proceeds we will instill into them a respect for American democracy and make easier the post-war education and management of their country as well as the rest of Europe that has been so long under Axis domination."[52]

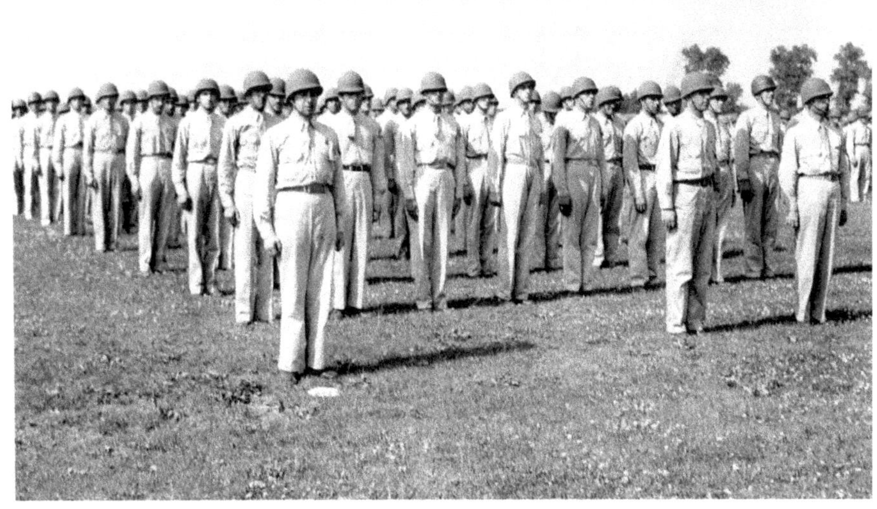

Italian Service Unit members in a drill formation at Camp Perry. *Courtesy of the Ottawa County Historical Museum, Peggy Debien, curator.*

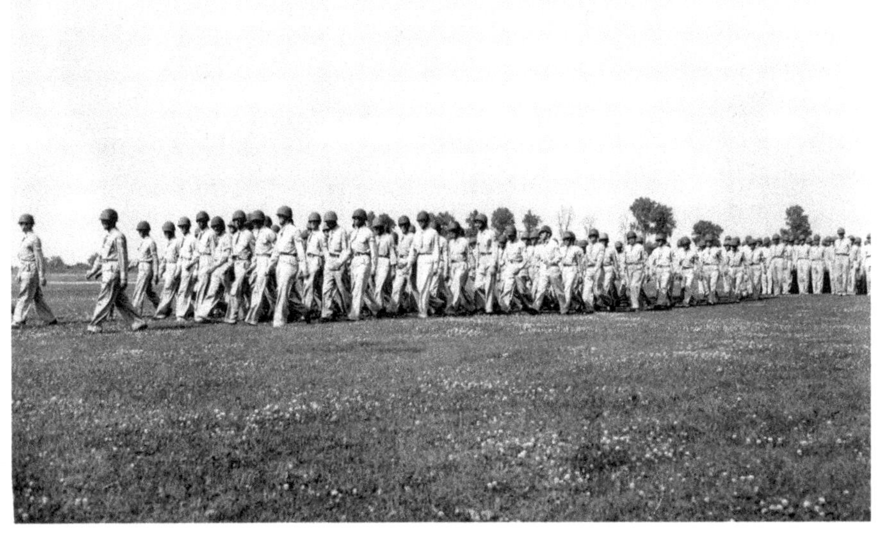

Italian Service Unit members in drill exercises at Camp Perry. *Courtesy of the Ottawa County Historical Museum, Peggy Debien, curator.*

ARRIVAL OF GERMAN PRISONERS OF WAR

The first several hundred Germans arrived on June 2, 1944. Italians who had signed up for ISU were placed in separate parts of the camp under the command of American officers, while non-ISU Italians were transferred to another camp. The Germans who arrived were between the ages of sixteen and forty and were familiar with their rights and privileges of the Geneva Convention. At this time, there were no German officers arriving at camp, although there were several noncommissioned officers. The first German prisoners of war were former Rommel Afrika Korps members and exhibited Nazi spirit. These prisoners were unwilling to be photographed out of fear that the photographs might be used for American propaganda purposes (Italian prisoners of war, meanwhile, welcomed being photographed). One reporter expressed, "After months in America, away from all, their eyes still expressed the desire to go back and join the fight for Germany."[53] The June 2, 1944 *Port Clinton Herald and Republican* article indicated that the Italian prisoners of war would be available for gardening and food processing work in the Port Clinton, Ohio area.[54]

The next arrival of German prisoners of war occurred on July 7, 1944, when the Germans were also organized into military units that included battalions and companies with American commanding officers. The companies were staffed with German first sergeants, company clerks, supply clerks and noncommissioned mess officers. The German prisoners had their own bakery, shoe repair shop, barbershop, two canteens and carpentry shop supervised by American officers. The German prisoners were allowed to keep their own uniforms until these eventually wore out; they were then replaced by salvaged American uniforms. The Germans had pride in wearing the Afrika Korps cap and would remake them when they wore out, an indication that there remained a number of hardcore Nazis that made every effort to control their fellow prisoners under the radar of the American officers.[55]

The Germans disliked the American 3.2 percent beer, which sold for ten cents a bottle, because its taste was too light. They could also buy Coca-Cola for four cents, Spuds cigarettes for fourteen cents and a copy of the *New York Times* for four cents on weekdays or twelve cents on Sundays. Rows of empty cases of Coca-Cola evidenced their preference for the soft drink, which was popular under the same name in Germany. Profits from the stockade canteens went to benefit the canteen.[56]

The next arrival of Germans occurred on September 8, 1944, when several hundred arrived from France. This wave of prisoners was assigned to agricultural labor projects within a fifty-mile radius of Camp Perry. The prisoners, who were still wearing their German uniforms when captured by U.S. troops, ranged in age from sixteen to forty. There were no officers in this group of prisoners of war.[57]

In November 1944, the Germans became the sole occupiers of Camp Perry after the 310th Quartermaster Battalion ISU unit was transferred to the Rossford Ordnance Depot in Toledo, Ohio. After the relocation of this unit, the only other ISU remaining in northern Ohio was at the Erie Proving Ground.[58]

The final group of German prisoners of war arrived on August 3, 1945. This group consisted of one thousand members of the German navy sent out to meet farm labor shortages in Ohio and northern Indiana. The influx of these German prisoners, who arrived from Camp McCain, Mississippi, meant that there were now close to six thousand prisoners of war under Camp Perry command working on farms and in local industries throughout Ohio. The majority of these new prisoners of war were assigned to the Camp Perry branch camps at Cambridge, Celina, Bowling Green, Defiance, Marion, Parma, Wilmington and Fort Wayne, Indiana.[59] German prisoners of war officers were allowed to wear their medals (as seen in the accompanying photo of a German officer at Camp Perry[60]) and did not have to engage in any work activities. The enlisted men were required to work and do periodic forced marches.

The Germans took pride in their cooking and used recipes from their homeland, as indicated by a reporter from the *Ottawa County News* on September 22, 1944:

> *It happened that as I was passing two huge ovens, a prisoner-baker opened the door of one oven. The smell was something that cannot be described. I got the prisoner to open the door a couple more times, and sensing my pleasure at the aroma, he grinned. In the oven reopened was a huge piece of pastry. Over it the prisoner was sprinkling cinnamon. The cake itself must have been fully a yard long and two feet wide. "That's streusel kuchen," the prisoner volunteered. "Smell good, eh?" For a fleeting moment I was tempted to remain behind and become a voluntary prisoner—at least until the kuchen was completely baked and sampled but I did get a taste of.*[61]

The prisoners of war, pursuant to the Geneva Convention, were required to receive the same food as their captors' army. The camp was under a

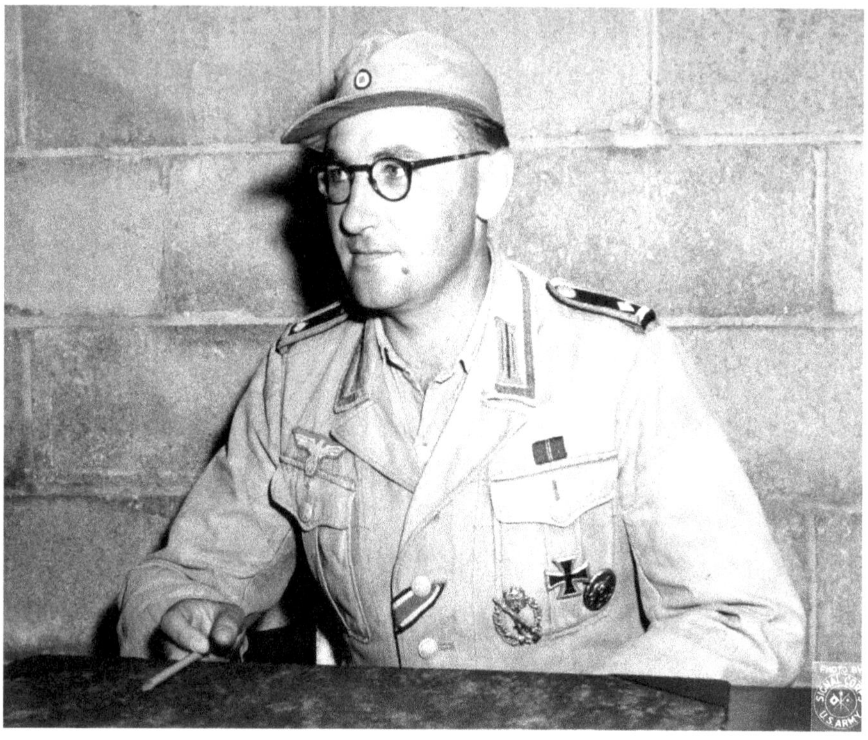

German officer at Camp Perry. *Courtesy of the Ottawa County Historical Museum, Peggy Debien, curator.*

rationing system, but it does not appear it was as limited as one might expect, especially as it pertained to available rations such as meats, poultry, canned goods and other foodstuffs which for the civilians was limited under their rationing system.[62]

The work performed by prisoners of war for their own benefit, such as working in the kitchens and mess halls, was considered unpaid work but could be elevated to paid work if the camp commandant considered it "necessary work." Food for the prisoners working in industries such as foundries was classified as "heavy work," and those prisoners would receive extra food at lunch. The prisoners of war had their own bakery and supplied the kitchens with fresh bread and pastries. Supplemental rations were supplied to the kitchens from the camp vegetable gardens. Overall, it appears that Camp Perry was able to provide adequate meals with the assistance of the prisoner of war labor, which was essential because of the civilian labor shortage.

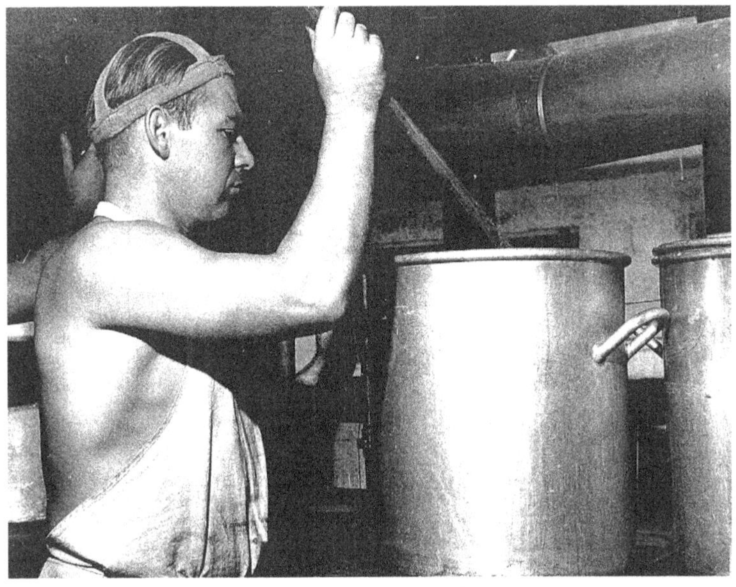

German prisoner of war stirring soup. *Courtesy of the NARA Photo: 208-AA-310-F-1.*

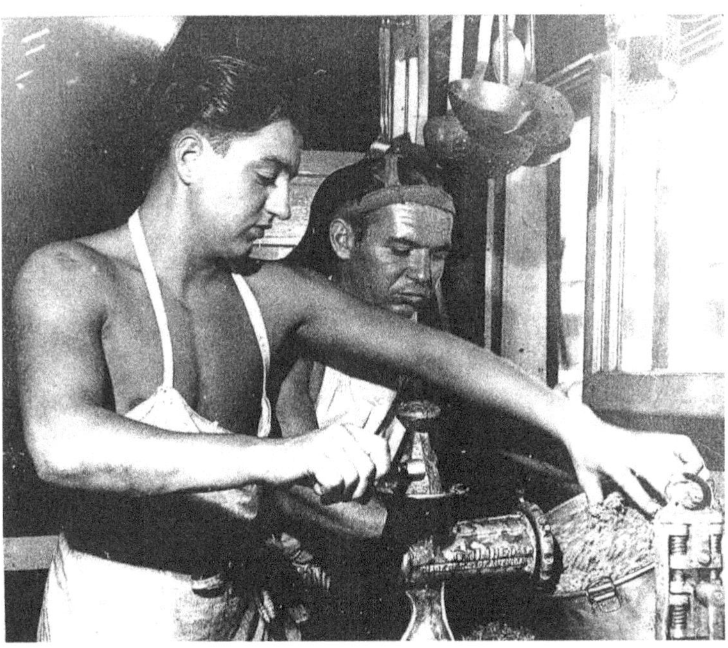

German prisoners of war grinding meat at Camp Perry. *Courtesy of NARA Photo: 208-AA-310-F-3.*

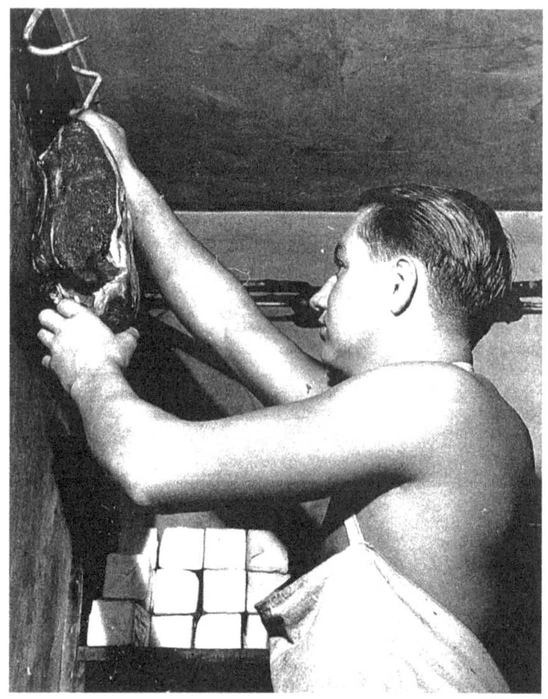

German prisoners of war in a refrigerator with meat hung in rows at Camp Perry. *Courtesy of NARA Photo: 208-AA-310-F-5.*

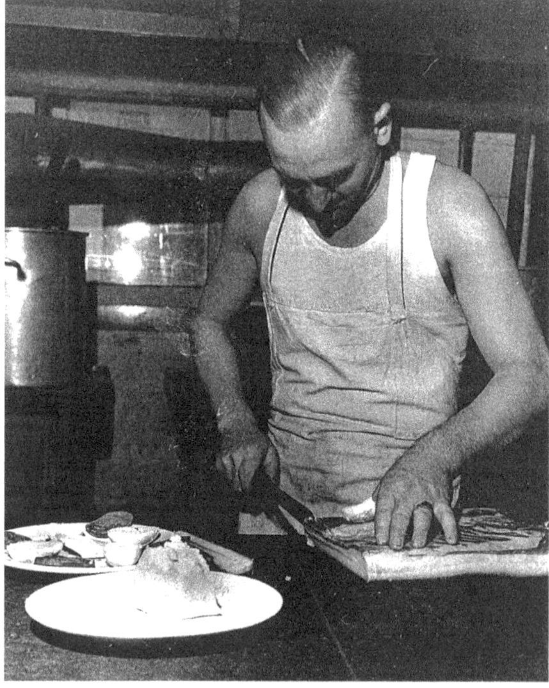

German prisoner of war preparing meals at Camp Perry. *Courtesy of NARA Photo: 208-AA-310-F-6.*

OBSERVATIONS

Camp Perry, with its branch camps, accommodated more than six thousand prisoners of war, who lived in hutments of five persons each. At the camps, the prisoners of war received the same food and medical care as any American soldier did, which irritated many Americans, especially since they were under a rationing system for food and name-brand products. They were most resentful, however, that the military was coddling the same enemy who had killed or captured their relatives overseas. The prisoners of war at Camp Perry installations were used to alleviate labor shortages in all areas, especially at local farms, where prisoners were transported daily to pick and package farm products. Under the leadership of Lieutenant Colonel E.C. McCormick Jr., the prisoners of war were assured adequate food, lodging and recreational activities that met the articles of the Geneva Convention.

3

ERIE PROVING GROUND

The Erie Proving Ground, covering more than 1,400 acres, was six miles west of Port Clinton, Ohio, adjacent to Camp Perry. It was a major player in reconditioning and shipping weapon systems and armor overseas during World War II. The accompanying photo shows what is left of the proof-firing locations used to test the mobile artillery. An *Ottawa County News* article entitled "Post-War Role Is Slated for Proving Ground" in the May 11, 1945 edition stated that the Erie Proving Ground proof-fired and shipped overseas 70 percent of the mobile artillery for the United States and its allies. More than 90,000 artillery units of all calibers were shipped from the Erie Proving Ground, the greatest volume of artillery ever shipped from an installation in U.S. history. For more than three years, an average of 50 railroad carloads and 70 truckloads were shipped daily over fourteen miles of track from a warehouse covering more than 17 acres. On one memorable Sunday, when the Germans' counterattack started the famous Battle of the Bulge on the western front, 117 carloads went out in a single day. By the end of the war, 70 percent of all the mobile artillery (200,000 units) used by the United States and the Allies under the lend-lease program were shipped from the Erie Proving Ground.[63]

Due to the great productivity at the Erie Proving Ground, there followed a high volume of correspondence at the site. The 1945 third-quarter historical report for the Erie Proving Ground recorded approximately 87,214 pieces of mail handled in the months of July, August and September—73,135 of

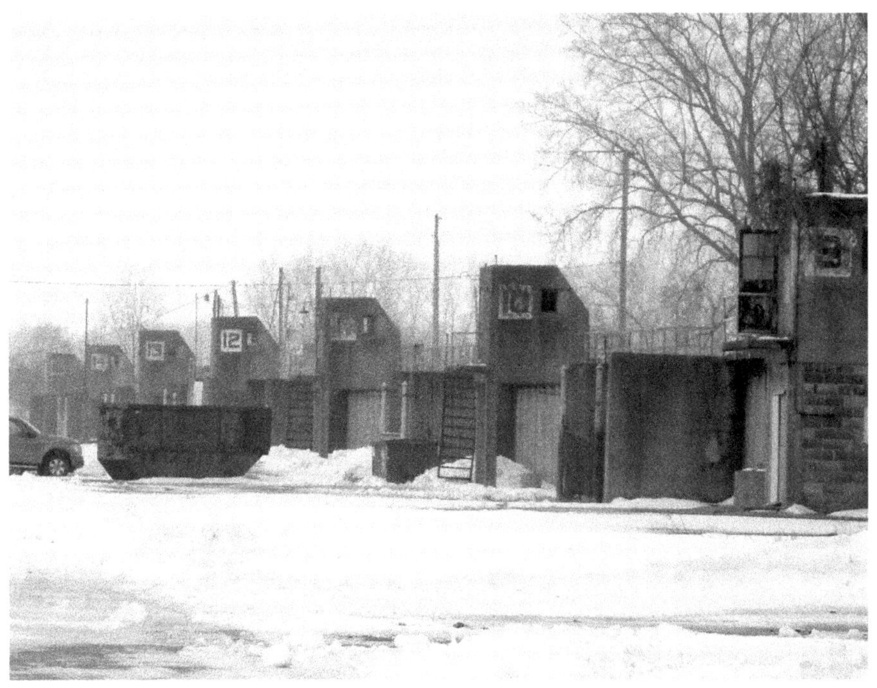

Former proof-firing locations at EPG. *Courtesy of the author's collection with the approval of Dublin Commercial Property Services, Inc.*

which was incoming and 13,079 outgoing. Another approximately 1,800 to 2,000 pieces of mail and intra-office papers were handled daily.[64]

The reproduction department was as busy as the mail department. Here they reproduced 572,245 copies of various documents during this same third quarter, further testimony that the Erie Proving Ground was working at peak levels during this time of the war. In what some might say true to form, the U.S. Army's bureaucracy descended upon the proving ground, requiring it to respond to 933 active government forms and 555 local reproduced forms distributed to the various divisions within the Erie Proving Ground.[65] This distribution was carried out at the administrative center, where the heads of the departments lived and coordinated the work of the more than five thousand civilians who stayed at the proving ground during the war. Above the entrance to the administrative center are three simulated burning flames engraved in stone that may have symbolized the burning flame of liberty emblematic of the Statue of Liberty. Another part of the administrative complex is the nearby firehouse, which is currently for sale and still appears structurally sound.[66]

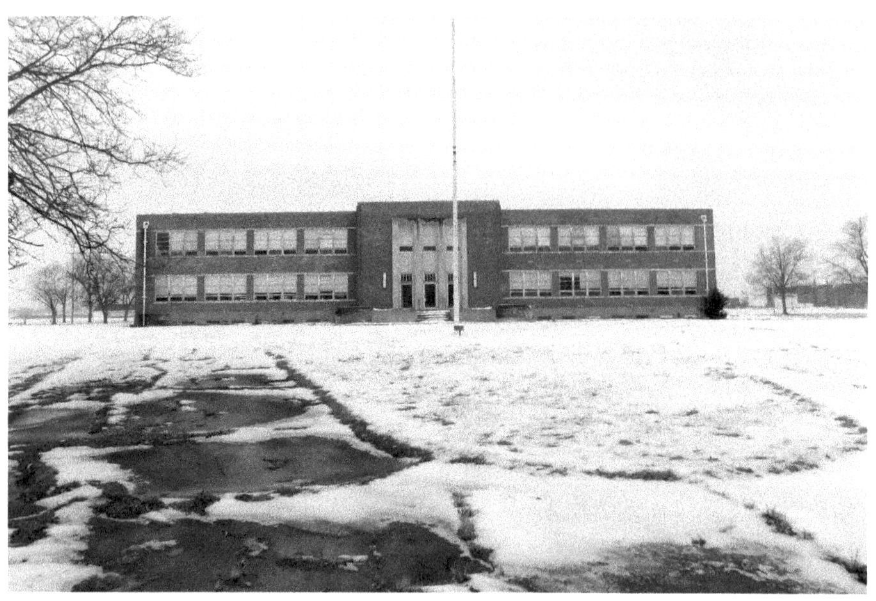

Former EPG administrative center. *Courtesy of the author's collection with the approval of Dublin Commercial Property Services, Inc.*

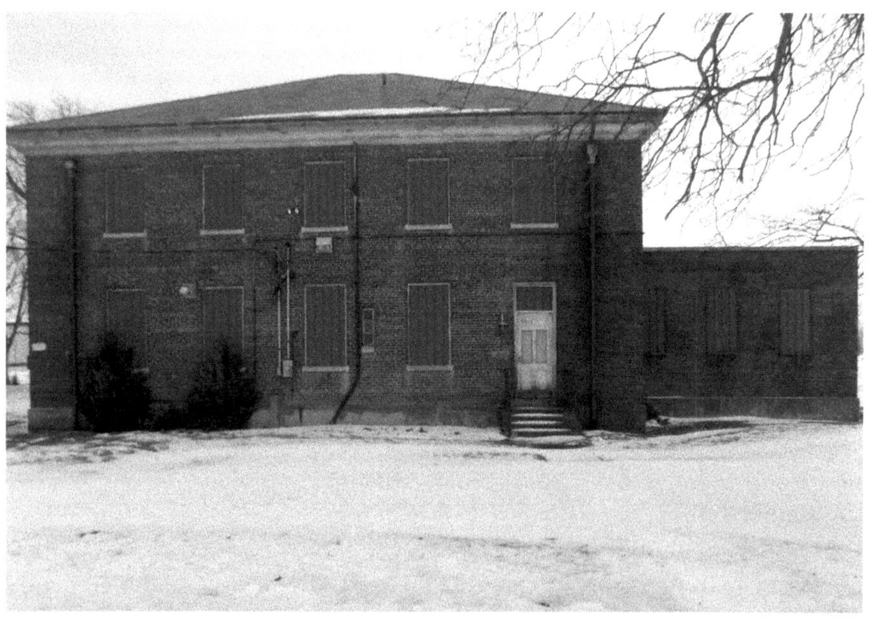

Former EPG firehouse. *Courtesy of the author's collection with the approval of Dublin Commercial Property Services, Inc.*

To meet the demand of reconditioning artillery equipment during World War II, there were more than five thousand civilians working at the Erie Proving Ground. To accommodate this large number of civilians, on-site buildings were renovated into dormitories, and new dormitories were built to house the workers and their families. A federal, prefabricated housing defense project known as Erie Gardens[67] was constructed on twenty-three acres of land in Port Clinton to house the proving ground employees and their families, in addition to other employees working in area defense projects. This complex of 259 two-family homes provided each family with four rooms of their own. Also, in Port Clinton, property owners were asked to assist in housing the war workers, given the high volume of work at the site.[68]

At the Erie Proving Ground, ISU members worked on salvaging and reconditioning 40-mm and 90-mm antiaircraft guns brought back from overseas in need of repair; they were not, however, involved in proof-firing the artillery. Italian prisoners of war worked side by side with the civilians working on chassis of antiaircraft guns.[69] The Italians also worked in the cafeteria, loaded and unloaded boxcars and built shipping cases. Eventually, all of the Italians left Camp Perry and were assigned to the Erie Proving

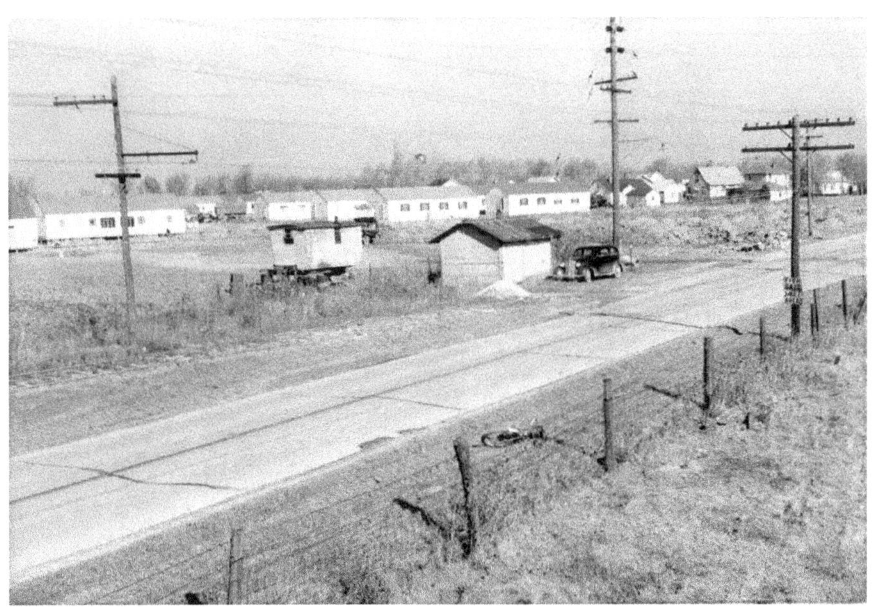

Erie Gardens in the 1940s. *Courtesy of the Ottawa County Historical Museum, Peggy Debien, curator.*

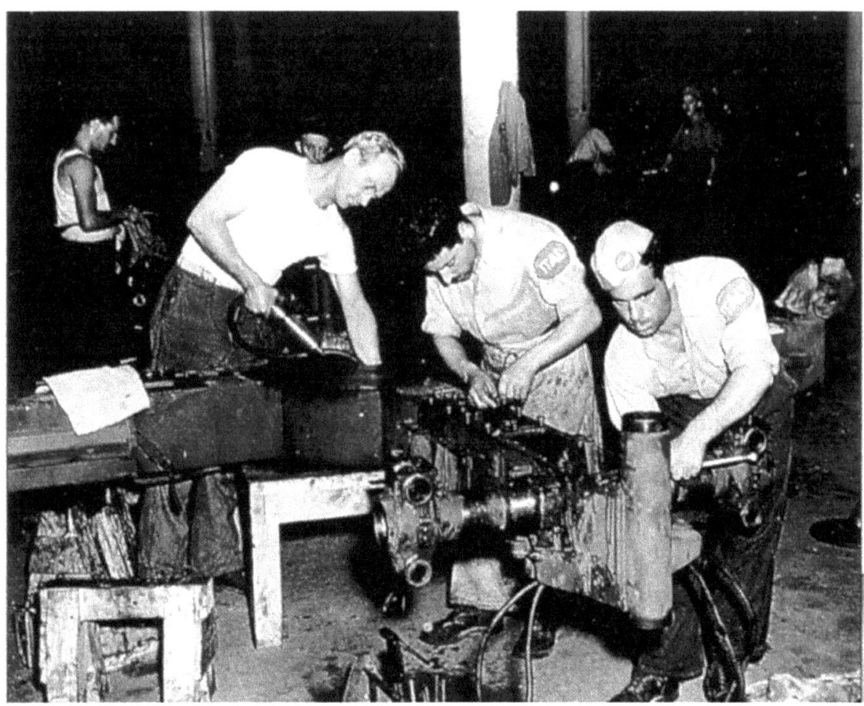

ASF. ORDNANCE DEPAR ENT, HQ., ERIE PROVING G UND, LACARNE, OHIO

IY AND BUY B NDS NOW FOR BYE AND BYE

Daily Bulletin

SAVE MANPOWER FOR WARPOWER, WORK SAFELY

NO. 155 MONDAY 2 July 1945

1. POST OFFICER OF THE DAY
   Today--------Lt.L.F.Deppensmith
   Tomorrow------Lt. G. S. Rideout
   Wednesday-----Capt. E. H. Bartell

2. STATION HOSPITAL OFFICER OF THE DAY
   Today--------Capt. L.H. Skimming
   Tomorrow-----Capt. V. W. Ritter
   Wednesday----Lt. B. C. Steele

3. ITALIAN QM BN DUTY OFFICER
   Today--------Lt. R. W. Hinton,III
   Tomorrow-----Lt. W. B. White
   Wednesday----Lt. J. E. Kiley

4. ECD DUTY OFFICER
   Today--------Lt. J. Aronsky
   Tomorrow----- Lt. H. Rood
   Wednesday----Capt. R. G. Farrell

5. PROOF DIVISION DUTY OFFICER
   Today--------Lt. M. J. Mance
   Tomorrow-----Lt. F. D. Whitehead Jr.
   Wednesday----Capt. C. Mantegani

6. SHOPS DIVISION DUTY OFFICER
   Today--------Capt. L. W. Perry
   Tomorrow-----Lt. W. H. Farmer
   Wednesday----Capt. W. P. Winchester

7. STORES DIVISION DUTY OFFICER
   Today--------Capt. L. R. Landis
   Tomorrow-----Lt. M. E. Gump
   Wednesday----Lt. M. E. Gump

8. TRANSPORTATION DIVISION N.C.O.
   Today-------- M/Sgt Tellier
   Tomorrow----- S/Sgt Frase
   Wednesday---- M/Sgt Tellier

By order of Colonel RUNDELL:

RAYMOND A. HOSKINS
WOJG USA
Asst. Adjutant

OFFICIAL:
Raymond A. Hoskins
RAYMOND A. HOSKINS
WOJG USA
Asst. Adjutant

1. ATTENTION ALL OFFICERS
   All officers and nurses are requested to submit their Immunization Registers, WD MD Form 81 or WD AGO Form 8-117, to the Military Personnel Branch in Building 201 in order that records may be brought up to date. Forms will be returned after information has been extracted. Hospital Personnel should submit their registers through the Hospital Adjutant.

2. MOVIE FOR TONIGHT
   "TWO O'CLOCK COURAGE" with Tom Conway and Ann Rutherford. Also Coney Island Honeymoon - Tee Tricks - Birthday Party - Technicolor Featurette-Sportscope - Little Lulu Cartoon.

SAFETY: There is no substitute for safety.

Above: Italian prisoners of war working with a civilian on the chassis of a 40-mm antiaircraft gun at the Erie Proving Grounds. *Courtesy of the Ottawa County Historical Museum, Peggy Debien, curator.*

Left: July 2, 1945 daily bulletin at EPG. *Courtesy of the NARA Box 8.*

Ground and to other branch camps, including the Rossford Ordnance Depot. At the peak of the war effort, there were one thousand ISU members working side by side with the civilians. Early on, it was decided that ISU members could work at the Erie Proving Ground since they had become co-belligerents, as opposed to the German prisoners of war, who still—in some cases—had a hatred of the United States and would do anything to sabotage its war efforts. To accommodate the assigned 323rd Italian Quartermaster Battalion, there were more than two hundred barracks, numerous mess halls and latrines evenly spaced between the barracks, in addition to a movie theater and canteen dedicated to the prisoners of war.

The *Daily Bulletin* listed the duty officers, including those assigned to the 323rd Italian Quartermaster Battalion unit, and announced the movies for the evening available to army personnel. It is also evident, given the type of work being done at the Erie Proving Ground, that safety was of paramount importance, as captured by the slogan "There is no substitute for safety."[70]

ENVIRONMENTAL CONCERNS

A number of environmental concerns have been raised about the Erie Proving Ground, as it was known from 1941 to 1951, or the Erie Army Depot, as it was called from 1951 to 1966, given the amount of ordnance fired over this time into Lake Erie. In 1967, the Erie Army Depot was closed and eventually turned into an industrial park. The large amount of ordnance proof-fired during World War II undoubtedly left a negative impact on the waters of Lake Erie. In fact, a U.S. Army Corps of Engineers (Louisville District) report stated that the corps has removed more than eight thousand non-explosive items and more than fourteen hundred potentially explosive items.[71] There are still occasions when ordnance is spotted in shallow waters or washes up on beaches near the old Erie Proving Ground location.

A Northwest Ohio EPA report highlights another environmental concern stemming from work done at the Erie Proving Ground during World War II that involved a landfill at the site. The report reads in part, "Contaminants known and suspected in Lake Erie and the surrounding soil are directly related to chemicals used in the production and firing of ordnance."[72] These findings raise the question of what the aftereffects were for the more than five thousand civilian employees who worked at the site from 1941 to 1946. Did they encounter negative reactions to the chemicals used in the production and firing of the ordnance, and could the exposures have caused health problems that may have led to hospitalizations or even deaths?

Of greatest concern today is determining which, if any, of the buildings were constructed on the landfill and any resulting negative health effects for employees from possible exposure. EPA guidelines state: "By their nature, munitions and explosives of concern (MEC) (including unexploded ordnance, buried munitions, and reactive or ignitable soil) may present explosive, human health, and/or environmental risks."[73] Such a landfill is in essence a burial pit that may contain a potent mixture of used, unused and fired munitions that could potentially explode or pose serious environmental risks if chemicals were to leech into the soil.

OBSERVATIONS

There are still buildings from the Erie Proving Ground era being used as warehouses; empty buildings that are vacant still look to be useable.[74] A building on the proving ground site—now the Lake Erie Industrial Park—has a "Danger—Keep Out—Danger—Chlorine" sign that leads one to question whether there are other buildings in the industrial park that carry similar danger signs and, if so, what steps are being taken to monitor the hazardous waste inside the buildings.

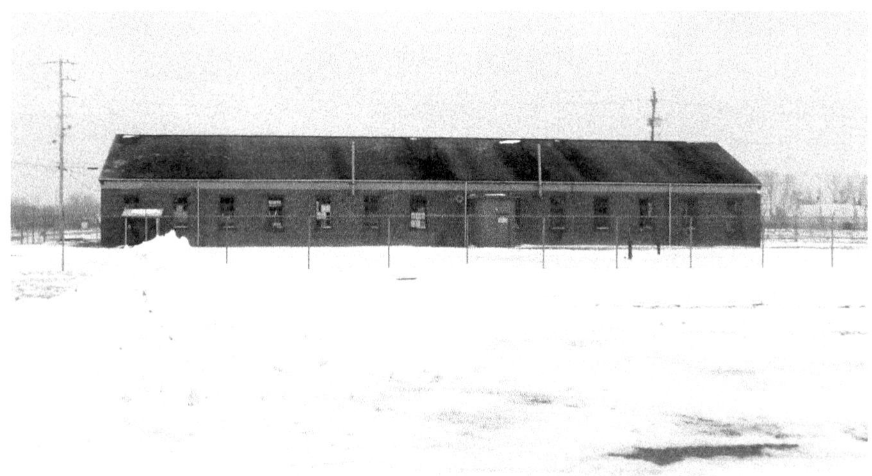

Former work site now used for storage. *Courtesy of the author's collection with the approval of Dublin Commercial Property Services, Inc.*

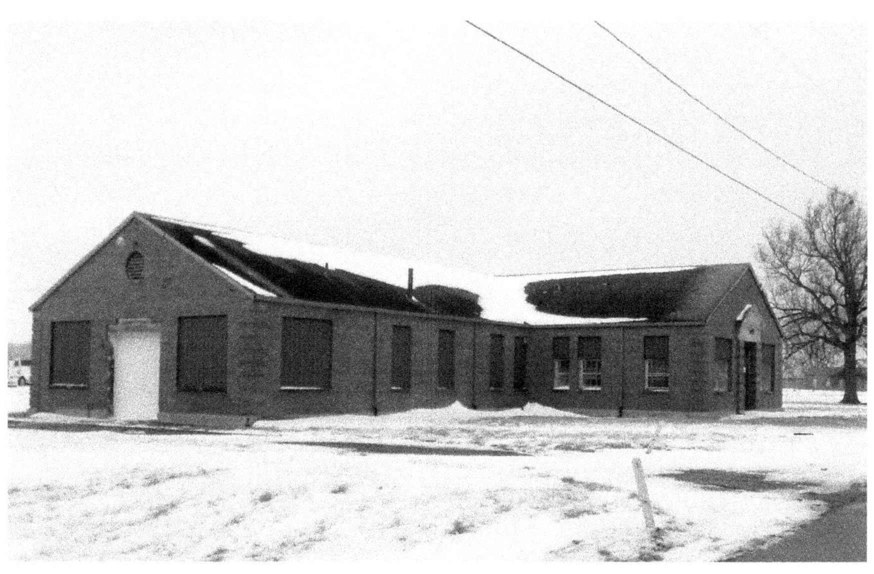

Former work site now used for storage. *Courtesy of the author's collection with the approval of Dublin Commercial Property Services, Inc.*

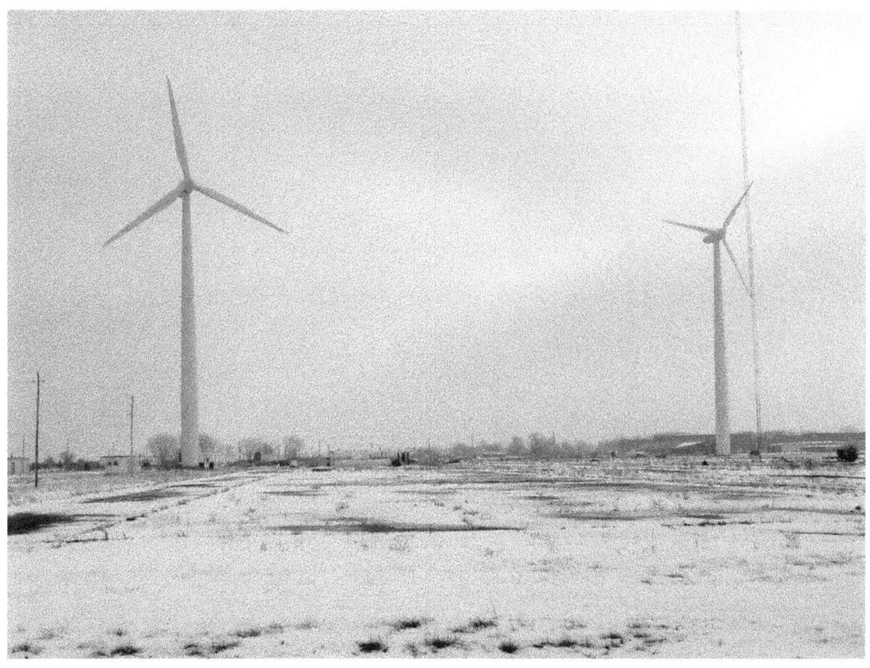

Wind turbines at the industrial park. *Courtesy of the author's collection with the approval of Dublin Commercial Property Services, Inc.*

Despite the vacant land and unoccupied buildings scattered throughout the industrial park, there are some active businesses on the property, including a company that develops and tests weapons systems in designated impact areas. A small wind farm operation, as seen in the accompanying author's photo,[75] has also taken root to produce energy-efficient power for the businesses that inhabit the park.

4

CAMP PERRY ENCAMPMENT

The first Italian prisoners of war came from the New York Central main line to the camp in October 1943 and were most likely greeted by a strong military presence. The prisoners of war were housed in one-story, tar-framed, five-man hutments measuring sixteen feet by sixteen feet on concrete slabs that once housed rows of tents. The inspection report of January 13–15, 1944, outlines the physical makeup of the camp.

> *This camp is located on the Military Reservation overlooking Lake Erie, in the northern part of the state of Ohio. Camp Perry was formerly the National Guard Camp for the State of Ohio and is now leased by the Federal Government. The Prisoner of War Camp is located on level terrain in about the center of the reservation. The tar paper-covered hutments present somewhat a drab appearance. The mess halls and latrines are constructed of concrete blocks. The prisoner of war hospital wards, with a capacity of one hundred five beds, are located adjacent to the station hospital at Camp Perry, a distance of approximately two miles.*[76] *The prisoners of war are housed in frame tar paper-covered hutments erected on concrete floors (pyramidal tents formerly erected over three floors when the camp was used by National Guard). Four to five prisoners are assigned to each hutment, which is heated by a small space heater, is well lighted and has sufficient air and floor space for the men housed. The interior of the hutments presents a very homely atmosphere and are well-policed. Steel cots are in use. The latrines and bathhouses in use in the stockade are*

of concrete block construction and appear to be sufficient for the prisoners of war with the exception of the laundry tub facilities with only sixteen tubs. There are eleven guard towers with small six-sided buildings atop of same and approximately level with top of fence are properly spaced to assure adequate control. The towers are heated with small space heaters but are not provided with searchlights or any means of emergency lighting of fence. One guard is on duty at all times, and no machine guns are in use in the towers. A single barbed wire fence, approximately nine feet high, consisting of nine strands of barbed wire, with no overhang, surrounds the stockade. The same type of fence surrounds the prisoner of war wards at the station hospital. The terrain is uniformly flat, and, therefore, there are no obstructions to the line of fire. Some of the buildings on the inside of the stockade such as the latrines, infirmary, school building, canteen and barbershop are within twenty feet of the fence. The nearest building on the outside of the fence is about seventy-five feet in distance. The New York Central Railroad has a spur within five hundred feet of the Stockade.

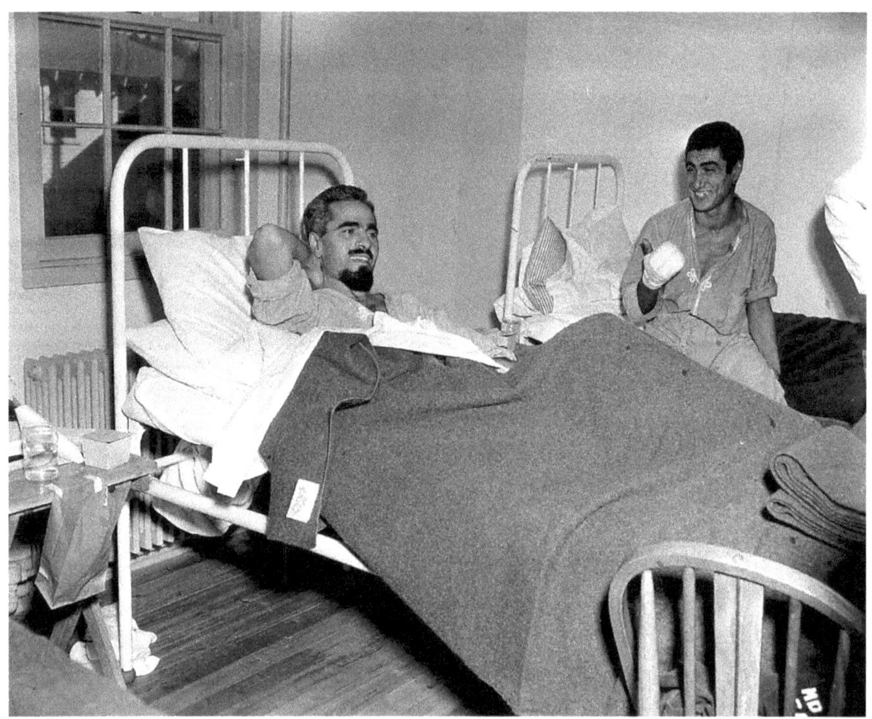

Italian POW in the hospital at Camp Perry. *Courtesy of NARA Photo 111-SC-38722.*

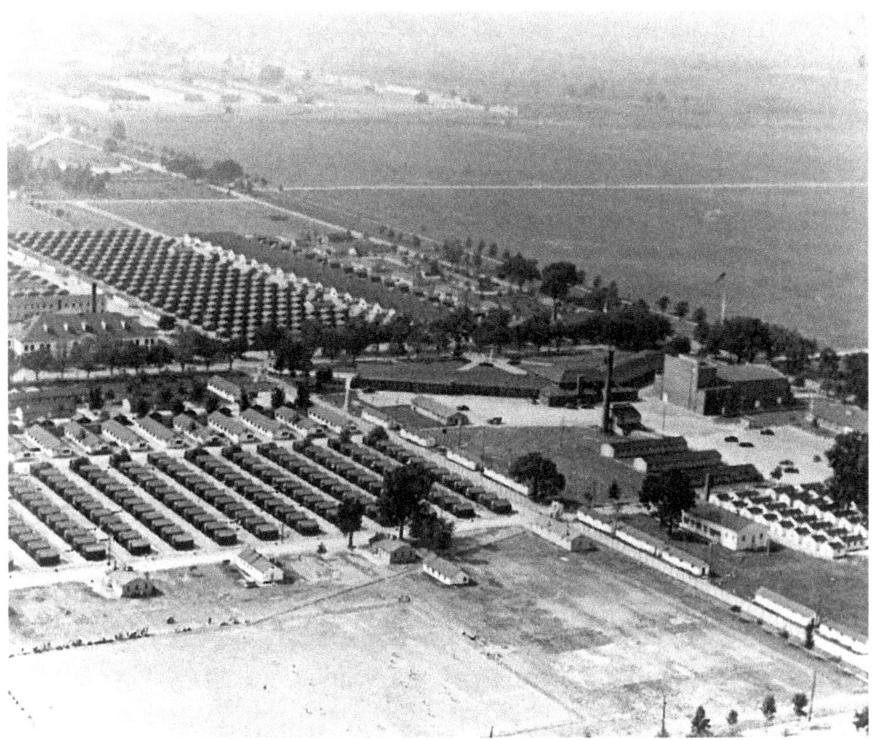

Italian and German hutments. *Courtesy of Ottawa County Historical Museum, Peggy Debien, curator.*

> *The nearest airport is an emergency landing field about ten miles west of Camp Perry. The Erie Proving Ground is located about two miles from the prisoner of war camp.*[77]

The physical makeup of the camp that originally housed only Italian prisoners of war was changed to house both Italian and German prisoners. An aerial view provides a picture of where the ISU was moved to the west beyond the central office area, while Germans were housed adjacent to the athletic field in twenty-seven rows of twelve hutments each (with five men per hutment) with mess halls directly to the west of the hutments.[78]

The remaining Italian hutments with concrete floors were once located near concrete block latrines and bathhouses that are no longer present on the western side of the camp. The hutments were winterized with woodstoves, had double walls and double paned windows and were later rehabbed to be used by the summer civilian marksmanship program until

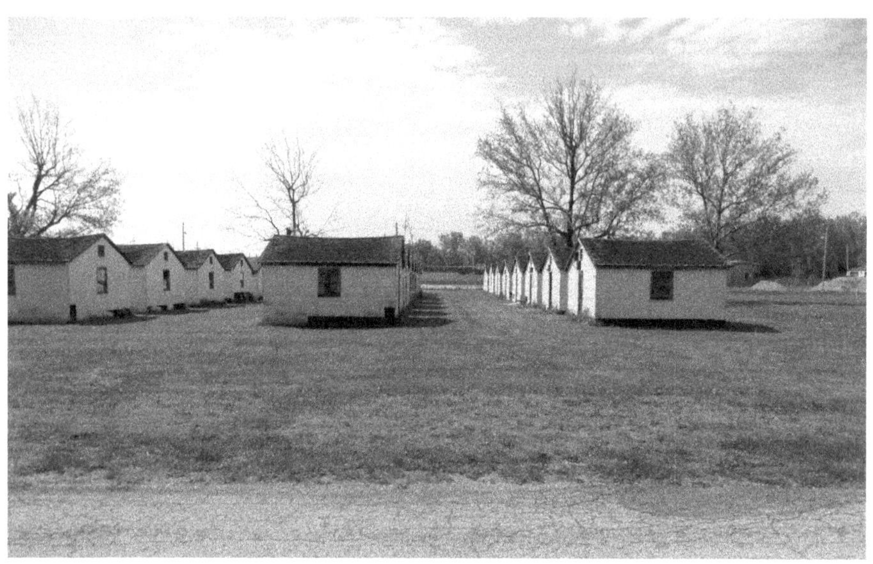

Italian hutments. *Courtesy of the author's collection with the approval of the Ohio National Guard and Camp Perry Joint Training Center.*

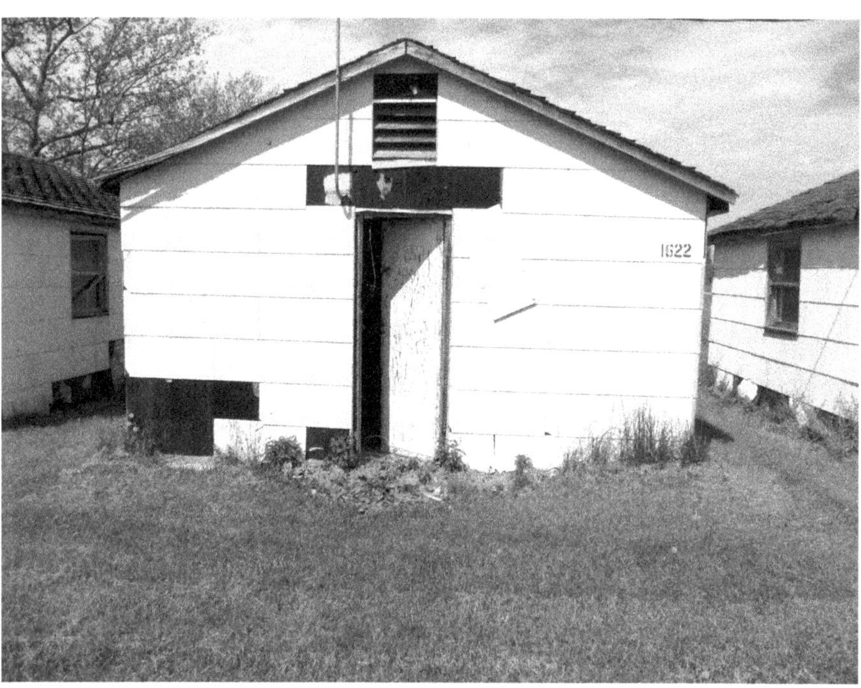

Italian hutment no. 1662 at Camp Perry. *Courtesy of the author's collection with the approval of the Ohio National Guard and Camp Perry Joint Training Center.*

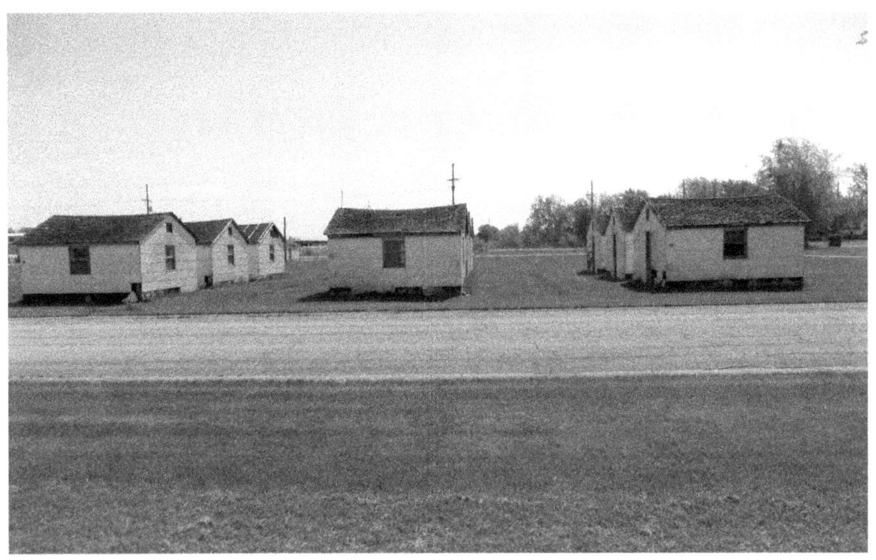

Remaining German hutments at Camp Perry. *Courtesy of the author's collection with the approval of the Ohio National Guard and Camp Perry Joint Training Center.*

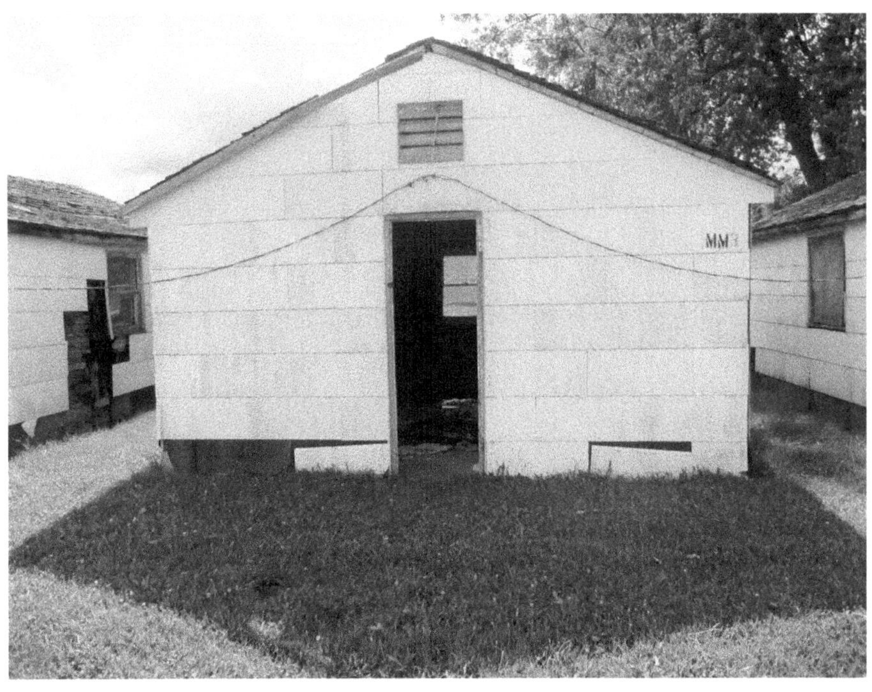

German hutment MM3 at Camp Perry. *Courtesy of the author's collection with the approval of the Ohio National Guard and Camp Perry Joint Training Center.*

just the past few years. In some cases, the latrines were located within twenty-five feet of the fence, while separate buildings housed laundry tubs for washing clothes.[79]

The remaining German hutments were located next to the athletic field, which now lies vacant, and so too are gone the concrete block latrines and bathhouses that were near the hutments. The Germans often decorated the interior of their hutments with paintings and, in some cases, pictures of Hitler and swastikas. The German hutments were arranged in a manner similar to the Italian hutments, with onetime concrete block latrines and bathhouses near the hutments. Just like the Italian hutments, the rehabbed German hutments were later used by the summer civilian marksmanship program until just a few years ago but appear to be in a state of more significant disrepair than the remaining Italian hutments.[80]

According to one of the last inspection reports dated August 17–20, 1945, Camp Perry had expanded to other branch camps that, taken together, allowed for the housing of 5,825 prisoners of war as detailed in the accompanying list:[81]

Base Camp	2,732
Branch Camps	
Defiance	237
Fort Wayne	901
Marion	520
Crile General Hospital (Parma)	295
Fletcher Hospital (Cambridge)	234
Columbus	450
Wilmington	126
Bowling Green	330
	5,825

CHART 8. Camp Perry and Branch Camps, POWs. *Courtesy of NARA, PMGO Inspection Reports-Perry, 1944.*

Some of Camp Perry's branch camps were temporary camps, including the camp at Celina, Ohio, with 294 German prisoners, and the camp at Defiance, Ohio, with 425 Germans. Both of these temporary camps were closed in October 1944, according to the October 5, 1944 Inspection

Report.[82] By all accounts, though, Camp Perry had the most extensive oversight of prisoners of war compared to all other prisoner of war camps in Ohio between 1943 and 1946.

CHANGING SEASONS

Measures were taken to ensure that the men were properly clothed as a means to prevent the spread of respiratory or communicable diseases, especially during winter's cold months along the shores of Lake Erie. The American officers were responsible for seeing that the prisoners of war had overcoats, raincoats, overshoes and caps. If a prisoner exceeded the allotted toilet paper articles for the month, he could purchase additional supplies at the canteen at his own expense. Rules were strictly enforced at Camp Perry; men were instructed that they had to sleep head to foot with quarters properly ventilated, the mess equipment properly sterilized and mess personnel required to report to the infirmary if they became infected by any kind of respiratory disease. Each company commander was told to set aside huts for housing sick prisoners of war as a means of quarantining those stricken with respiratory diseases, which was quite common in the camp due to its location on Lake Erie and the changing Midwest seasons, which often brought high winds off the lake. For those requiring additional medical care, a hospital was located nearby, where patients were treated by American doctors or, in some cases, by prisoner of war doctors.

The Inspection Report of October 6, 1944, indicated that the camp had its own infirmary, with more severe patients being transferred to the base hospital. On the day of the visit, there were forty-seven patients at the hospital, including some stricken with malaria and one transfer to a general hospital with a serious cranial fracture and a piece of metal placed over the wound.[83]

OBSERVATIONS

Camp Perry was an extensive operation that began with Italian prisoners of war and expanded to include Germans, with each group separated from each other by a roadway. The Italian prisoners of war were eventually

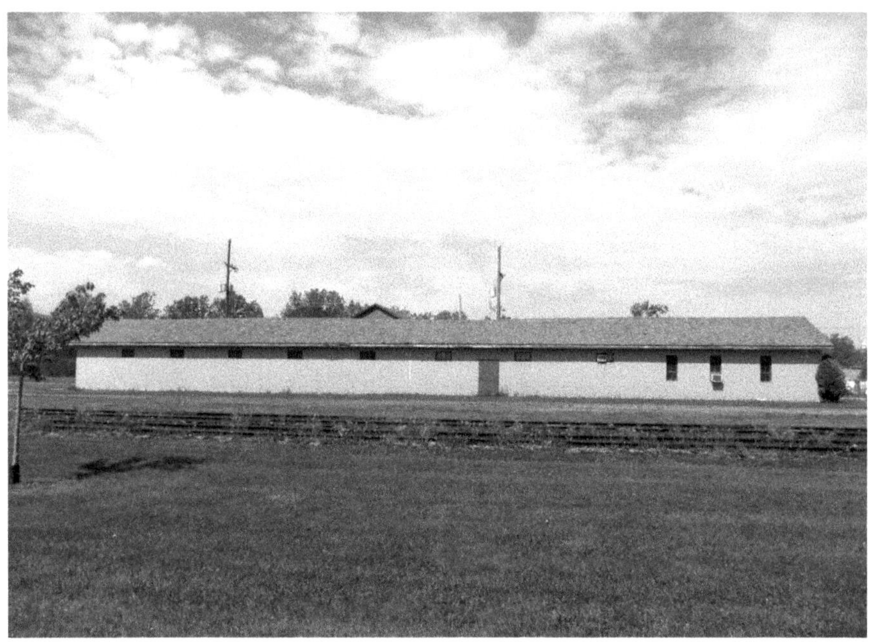

Old ammo storage depot converted to a storage facility at Camp Perry. *Courtesy of the author's collection with the approval of the Ohio National Guard and Camp Perry Joint Training Center.*

transferred to the Erie Proving Ground and to other branch camps, leaving only the German prisoners at the camp and leading to the expansion of canteens, movie theaters and other recreational facilities. After the camp closed, the hutments were used by the Ohio National Guard and civilian marksmanship programs through the 1990s. The old ammo storage depot has been converted into a storage facility.[84]

Chapter 3 highlighted the contamination issue that exists at the Lake Eire Industrial Park, and one can only imagine the kind of exposure for the prisoners of war who lived in the hutments at Camp Parry, which may have been constructed with cancerous materials such as asbestos. During World War II, products that were used in wallboard, shingles, roofing and cement board in construction of buildings were eventually linked to cancerous materials, especially if weakened or exposed to the elements. The question is whether or not the hutments later used by the Camp Perry constituents contained cancerous materials. There was not a sufficient understanding of the effect that cancerous chemicals had on human life. This is now being corrected through funds from the Formerly Used Defense Site (FUDS) program, which is removing hazardous materials from those sites.

5
CAMP PERRY RULES AND REGULATIONS

MILITARY DISCIPLINE AND COURTESIES

The first prisoners of war to arrive at Camp Perry were the one thousand Italians who entered the camp on October 10, 1943. Less than one month later, on November 2, 1943, Major E.C. McCormick Jr., the camp commandant, issued Memorandum No. 12 in order to establish the military discipline and courtesies for the prisoners at the camp.[85] The orders were the following:

> *Discipline*
> *Prisoners of War are subject to the laws, regulations, and orders in force in the Army of the United States, including the Articles of War, Subject to exceptions and qualifications prescribed by law, International agreement, or by War Department, Prisoners of War are within the jurisdiction of court-martial and are liable to summary punishment by officers of the Army of the United States. Prisoners of War are also subject to the civil laws of the United States and of the state and municipality where interned.*
>
> *Noncommissioned officers and other designated leaders who fail to properly perform duties of supervision of men under them, or any other duty with which they are entrusted, will be punished against good order and discipline.*
>
> *Each Prisoner of War is responsible for government property and clothing issued to him and will be chargeable in event of its loss or damage other than reasonable wear. Each Prisoner of War is also responsible for other*

governmental property lost or damaged because of misconduct. Inspections will be made from time to time and the cost of any damaged or lost or damaged by misconduct will be charged against the responsible Prisoners of War. Indebtedness so incurred will be collected from current allowance and compensation for work.

Prisoners of War will at all times show the utmost respect toward American officers and noncommissioned officers as well as their own Italian officers and noncommissioned officers. Orders from all officers and noncommissioned officers will be obeyed willingly and promptly.

Prisoners of War will be in attendance at Reveille and Retreat unless excused for medical reasons.

Courtesies

When the National Anthem is played or To the Colors, Escort of Colors, or Retreat is sounded, Prisoners of War not in building will stand at attention and face the music or Colors.

In addition to the courtesies required by regulations in force in the Italian army regarding officers, Prisoners of War will salute all noncommissioned officers of the United States Armed Forces.

A Prisoner of War in a military formation will not salute unless he is command thereof.

A Prisoner of War out of doors upon the approach of an officer will face toward at attention and salute. Prisoners of War assigned work will not salute an officer unless addressed by him.

When an officer enters a room in which there are Prisoners of War, the latter will stand at attention and uncover until the officer indicates otherwise.

When an officer enters a mess hall Prisoners of War will remain seated, continue eating, but will not converse.

On entering a room where an officer is present the Prisoner of War will uncover.

Before addressing an Officer, a Prisoner of War will salute. He also will salute upon termination of the interview.

A Prisoner of War in ranks will assume the position of attention when addressed by an officer.

The content of this directive will be brought to the attention of all Prisoners of War at this camp. This regulation will be posted in a non-conspicuous place in all orderly rooms, and on all bulletin boards.

Necessary disciplinary measures will be taken in the case of any action inconsistent with and in violation of the content of this directive.

The camp announced to the prisoners of war that violation of the military discipline and courtesies order could lead to prisoner confinement and the receiving of only one piece of bread and one quart of water per meal. While in confinement, prisoners of war were not allowed to sing or talk, nor were they allowed to open any door in the block to watch passersby. Infraction of the rule would lead to an additional day of confinement, plus the need for guards to escort them to the latrine. While in confinement, prisoners of war were allowed to keep the clothes they had and were given the basic necessities: two blankets, one pair of socks, one raincoat, one bar of soap, one tube of shaving cream, one tube of toothpaste, one comb, one suit of underwear, one towel, one razor (with blades being turned into the prison office and furnished as needed) and one toothbrush. The hutment was sparsely furnished, with only a steel bed with no mattress and blankets provided at night. The lights had to be out at 2100 (9:00 p.m.), and neither reading materials nor cigarettes were allowed. Each morning, a prison officer checked the hutments for any prohibited articles. If a prisoner of war came near the confinement areas, he would be subject to disciplinary action.[86]

LIST OF CALLS

E.C. McCormick Jr. set down the accompanying list of calls for the Italian prisoners of war in Memorandum No. 4A on October 12, 1943. Twenty-four-hour clock times have been added for reference:[87]

Type Call		Weekdays	Sundays
Bugle	Reveille, First Call	0530 (5:30 a.m.)	0630 (6:30 a.m.)
Whistle	Assembly	0600 (6:00 a.m.)	0700 (7:00 a.m.)
Bugle	Mess Call (Breakfast)	0605 (6:05 a.m.)	0705 (7:05 a.m.)
Whistle	Assembly	0645 (6:45 a.m.)	
Bugle	Sick Call	0700 (7:00 a.m.)	0800 (8:00 a.m.)
Bugle	Church Call	0900 (9:00 a.m.)	
Bugle	Recall	1130 (11:30 a.m.)	
Bugle	Mess Call (Dinner)	1200 (12:00 p.m.)	1200 (12:00 p.m.)
Whistle	Assembly	1245 (12:45 p.m.)	
Bugle	Recall	1600 (4:00 p.m.)	
Bugle	Assembly	1655 (4:55 p.m.)	
Bugle	Retreat	1700 (5:00 p.m.)	

Type Call		Weekdays	Sundays
Bugle	Mess Call (Supper)	1715 (5:15 p.m.)	1715 (5:15 p.m.)
Bugle	Tattoo	2100 (9:00 p.m.)	2100 (9:00 p.m.)
Whistle	Call to Quarters	2145 (9:45 p.m.)	2145 (9:45 p.m.)
Whistle	Taps	2200 (10:00 p.m.)	2200 (10:00 p.m.)

CHART 9. List of Calls. *Courtesy of Memorandum 4A, October 12, 1943.*

The list of calls represents the daily sequence of bugle and whistle calls that signaled the announced schedule of events for the prisoners of war, a sequence similar to the bugle and whistle calls performed at U.S. military installations. The prisoner of war's day at Camp Perry started with a wake-up call of **Reveille**, followed by an **Assembly** of the prisoners in one location before being called to **Mess** for a forty-minute breakfast. The prisoner returned to **Assembly** with a **Sick Call** fifteen minutes later, with the rest of the prisoners of war going about their business at the camp. A ceasing of morning activities was announced at **Recall**, when prisoners returned to their hutments just before lunch, followed one half hour later by a **Mess Call** that signaled a forty-five-minute lunch, and then a return to **Assembly** before being dismissed for afternoon activities. An afternoon **Recall** was performed to signal the end of afternoon activities and for the prisoners of war to return to their hutments, with another **Assembly** forty-five minutes later. At this time, they participated in the evening **Retreat**, defined in the November 2, 1943 Memorandum No. 12 under the section, "Courtesies": "When the National Anthem is played or to the Colors, Escort of Colors, or Retreat is sounded, Prisoners of war not in a building will stand at attention and face the music of Colors." After the **Retreat,** which signaled the end of the day, the prisoners of war proceeded to dinner, followed at 2100 (9:00 p.m.) by a bugle call or music prior to **Call to Quarters**, which signaled to the prisoners that they were not to be absent from their hutments for the night. The end of the day occurred when **Taps** was played, indicating that all lights needed to be extinguished.

The next day followed the same sequence of bugle and whistle calls, but Sunday mornings marked a more flexible schedule, with prisoners receiving one extra hour of sleep. The list of calls was similar at Camp Perry's branch camps and at the outside contact work areas, where the prisoners had to follow a similar pattern and regimented schedule.

It was evident that the prisoners of war were held to a rigid military schedule of events, including a time at the end of the day for Retreat, when

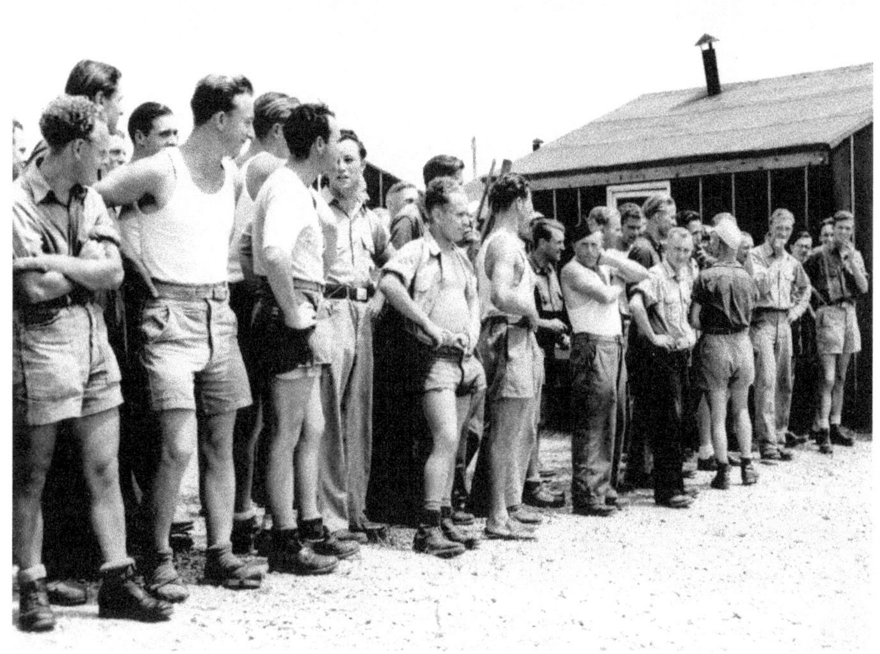

Italian prisoners of war at assembly at Camp Perry. *Courtesy of the Ottawa County Historical Museum, Peggy Debien, curator.*

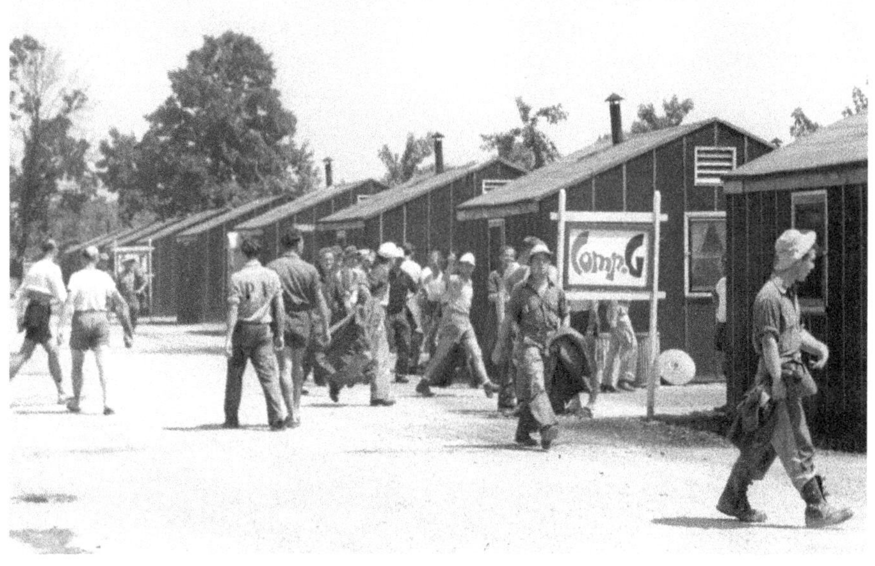

Prisoners of war in retreat at Camp Perry. *Courtesy of the Ottawa County Historical Museum, Peggy Debien, curator.*

the prisoners were required to stand at attention during the national anthem or when the color guard put their evening-ending ceremonies to music. The photos depict Italian prisoners of war at Assembly and Recall.[88] A count was taken in the morning at Reveille of those prisoners present and those in the hospital, and a similar evening count was taken at Retreat to ensure that no prisoners of war went missing.

VISITORS

The camp developed a protocol for accepting visitors, with permission being granted by the camp commander that allowed prisoners to receive visitors twice a month. The visits were under the supervision of military personnel and within earshot of a military interpreter. In the beginning, when only Italian prisoners of war inhabited Camp Perry, the scope of the language interpreters was limited to English and Italian, with German being added after the German prisoners of war arrived. Visitors were required to be searched before and after each visit along with the prisoners of war. Any article denied to the visitor during the visit was deposited with an officer, and a receipt was given, with the article being returned upon the visitor producing the receipt before departing camp. The camp instituted a procedure for admitting visitors whereby the visitor was required to complete a form to start the visitation process. If accepted by the camp commander, the visitor was granted permission through an acceptance letter, and a record of the visit was set down according to date, time of arrival and departure, and those in attendance.[89]

GIFTS AND ACKNOWLEDGEMENT

A standard letter was used to acknowledge the receipt of gifts and for indicating that the gifts would be used for the benefit of all prisoners at the camp. This also reassured the sender that all interments were being treated humanely and were receiving the necessary clothing, food and shelter. The letter mentions that the majority of the interments were working in the areas of carpentry, plumbing, masonry and harvesting on nearby farms, and any question as to whether there were relatives among the group ought to be directed to the Prisoner of War Information Bureau in Washington, D.C.[90]

INCENTIVES

An incentive plan was developed to assist in the maintenance and policing of the hutments, latrines, mess halls, administration building and laundry room. The incentive plan was as follows:

> *One carton of cigarettes and honorary shield to the mess hall that had the best appearance as it pertained to organization and cleanliness.*
> *Five packages of cigarettes and honorary shield to the hutment within each company that had the best appearance.*
> *One carton of cigarettes and shield to be hung in the company street that had the highest number of honor points based on neatness of the administration building and other buildings in the company area.*

The incentive plan was also tied to the responsibilities of the prisoner of war companies to care for the recreation areas, unoccupied areas of the compound and the laundry and drying rooms, all of which were reviewed during weekly inspections by American officers, who followed established criteria to award prizes. It seems clear that the incentive plan was more difficult to implement among the German prisoners of war, given their overall hostile nature upon arriving at Camp Perry.[91]

OBSERVATIONS

One of the inspection reports—which in most cases were prepared by a representative from the Legation of Switzerland—indicates how impressed outside observers were with the administration and operation of the camp, as it pertained in particular to the close supervision of the prisoners of war. One observation stated: "The general atmosphere of the Camp is good. The discipline appears to be fairly strict but benevolent in tone."[92] The reports indicated that when the administrators of the camp encountered German prisoners of war who refused to follow the rules, they were transferred to other camps in an effort to isolate those hardcore Nazi sympathizers.

The February 13, 1945 Inspection Report stated: "There have been no escapes and no court-martial trials. In the side camps there is some political activity, especially at Marion which is known as a strong Nazi camp."[93] Later inspection reports leading up to the closing of Camp Perry continued the narrative that the camp rules and regulations were being followed, that discipline was firm and that there were on average about ten prisoners in the guardhouse at any one time for disciplinary problems, all of which reaffirm the reputation that Lieutenant Colonel E.C. McCormick Jr. and his staff at Camp Perry were firm, effective, but fair disciplinarians.

6

POSTAL SERVICE

The prisoners of war at Camp Perry were permitted to mail just one letter and one postcard per week. The length of the letter was restricted to one sheet of paper of twenty-four lines on one side, while a postcard was restricted to just nine lines. A letter written by the camp spokesman to military officials, government officials or aid and relief organizations was not restricted in length or number, however. The letterhead and outside of the envelope or postcard of each correspondence to or from a prisoner had to contain the prisoner's name, serial number, name of camp and language of the communication.[94] The translated prisoners of war correspondence are examples of how welcome the prisoners were to receiving and sending correspondence back home.

Letter from Alfred Dymann to his wife and daughter:[95]

Camp Perry, Ohio April 2, 1945

Dear Mom and Dolly,

I can inform you that I was very lucky this week. I received two letters, from January 2, 1944 and one from January 26, 1944. Besides the Christmas package also arrive in good condition.

Actually, I did not expect it yet. The bakery (Kuchen) was still remarkable good. I did not open the can yet. It appears to fine on the outside. I'm sure, it will be so on the inside, too. I will write more about it, once I open it. Thanks so much.

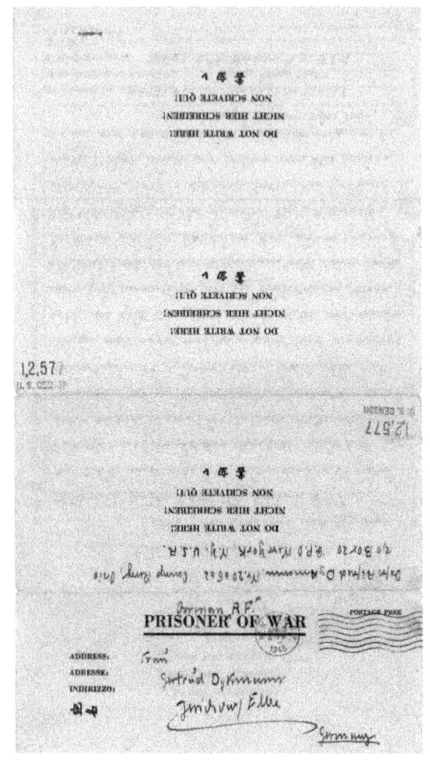

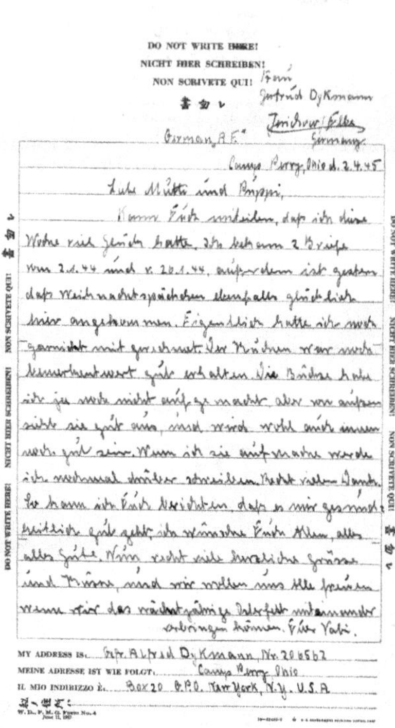

German prisoner of war Alfred Dymann's cover to letter (*left*) and letter (*right*) sent home to his family. *Courtesy of a purchase by the author at www.ebay.com.*

I can inform you, physically I am very well. I wish you all the very, very best.

Dearest of greetings and many kisses. And we all will be happy, if we will be able to celebrate next year's Easter's Holiday together.

Your Daddy

Letter from Werner Neubauer to his parents and sister:[96]

July 17, 1944.

Dear Parents and Sister,

Today, on Sunday, I want to send you greetings from a far-away country. I am still very well. I hope so are all of you. We work here on the farm. [Several lines redacted.]

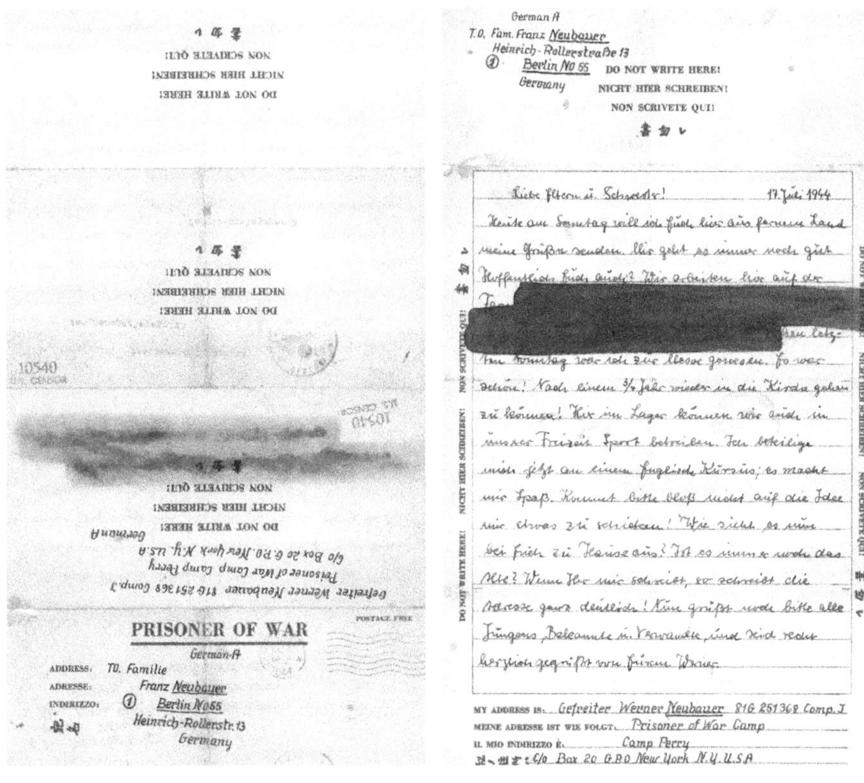

PRISONER OF WAR

POSTAGE FREE

ADDRESS: / ADRESSE: / INDIRIZZO:

German-A
TO. Familie
Franz Neubauer
① Berlin No55
Heinrich-Rollerstr. 13
Germany

German A
T.O. Fam. Franz Neubauer
Heinrich-Rollerstraße 13
① Berlin No 55
Germany

DO NOT WRITE HERE!
NICHT HIER SCHREIBEN!
NON SCRIVETE QUI!

Liebe Eltern u. Schwester! 17. Juli 1944

Heute am Sonntag will ich Euch hier aus fernem Land meine Grüße senden. Mir geht es immer noch gut. Hoffentlich Euch auch? Wir arbeiten hier auf der Fa[...] am letzten Sonntag war ich zur Messe gewesen. So war schön! Nach einem 3/4 Jahr wieder in die Kirche gehen zu können! Hier im Lager können wir auch in unserer Freizeit Sport betreiben. Ich beteilige mich jetzt an einem Englisch Kursus; es macht mir Spaß. Kommt bitte bloß nicht auf die Idee mir etwas zu schicken! Wie sieht es nun bei Euch zu Hause aus? Ist es immer noch das Alte? Wenn Ihr mir schreibt, so schreibt die Adresse ganz deutlich! Nun grüßt noch bitte alle Jungens, Bekannte u. Verwandte, und Euch recht herzlich gegrüßt von Eurem Werner.

MY ADDRESS IS: Gefreiter Werner Neubauer 81G 251368 Comp. I
MEINE ADRESSE IST WIE FOLGT: Prisoner of War Camp
IL MIO INDIRIZZO È: Camp Perry
c/o Box 20 G.P.O New York N.Y. U.S.A

German prisoner of war Werner Neubauer's cover to letter (*left*) and letter (*right*) sent home to his family. *Courtesy of Steve Cooper, general manager and marketing manager of the Civilian Marksmanship Program at Camp Perry.*

Last Sunday I went to Mass. It was nice to be able to go to church after ¾ of a year. Here in the camp we are able to participate in sports in our time-off. Right now, I am taking an English course; I like it. (It is fun)

Please do not get the idea to send anything!

How are things at home now? Is everything still the same?

When you write me to me, please write the address very clearly. Please give greetings to the boys, friends and relatives. Special greetings to you from your Werner

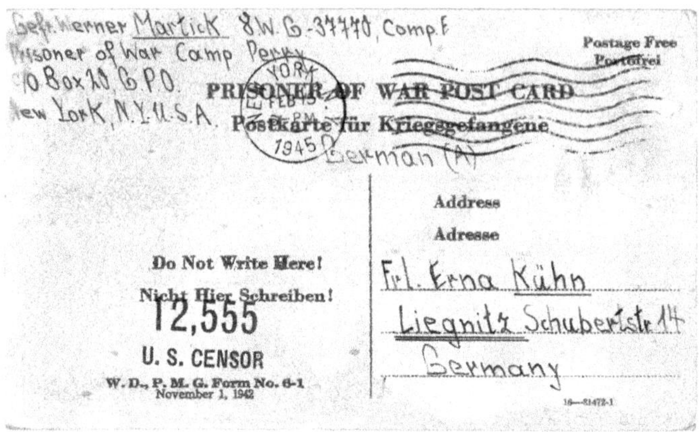

Gefr. Werner Martick 8W.G-37770, Comp. F
Prisoner of War Camp Perry
P.O. Box 20, G.P.O.
New York, N.Y. U.S.A.

PRISONER OF WAR POST CARD
Postkarte für Kriegsgefangene

German (A)

Postage Free
Portofrei

Do Not Write Here!
Nicht Hier Schreiben!

12,555
U. S. CENSOR

W. D., P. M. G. Form No. 6-1
November 1, 1942

Address
Adresse

Frl. Erna Kühn
Liegnitz Schubertstr. 14
Germany

16—81472-1

German prisoner of war Werner Neubauer's cover of postcard (*top*) and note (*bottom*) sent home to his family. *Courtesy of Steve Cooper, general manager and marketing manager of the Civilian Marksmanship Program at Camp Perry.*

Postcard from Werner Martick to his wife:[97]

February 8, 1944.

Dear Erna!

I can report (to you: formal address!) with great joy that I received mail from you for the first time. You can certainly imagine at home how happy I was. I regret, I am only able to write a little card. But, as soon as possible I will write a letter. You dear note from the month of December. I thank you again.

Greetings Werner

This correspondence of the three prisoners of war reveals how much they looked forward to receiving mail from home. The postcards were initially used by the prisoners as a means of framing their correspondence in a succinct manner so they would become accustomed to writing letters of only twenty-four lines.

The Werner Neubauer letter spoke of his work on a farm and the opportunities that Camp Perry provided the prisoners of war to participate in religious services, recreation activities and English courses, which both enabled the German prisoners to better communicate with their American captors and—in line with Camp Perry's re-education effort—gain a clearer understanding of the principles of democracy versus Nationalism Socialism.

Alfred Dymann expressed gratefulness for the food he received from home and provided reassurance to his family members that he was healthy and missed them dearly, as evidenced in his heartfelt passage, "Dearest of greetings and many kisses." Given that his letter was written on April 2, 1945, and from his hope that "we all will be happy, if we will be able to celebrate next year's Easter's Holiday together," it is evident that Alfred was longing for the war in Europe to end soon and to be back home with his family to celebrate the holidays with his wife and daughter. The war's end on May 7 would make Alfred's dream a reality.

The men were thankful for the letters and food they received from home, both of which helped keep them connected to their lives back home. The letters provided reassurances that their family members were still there for them and gave a positive spark to their lives of confinement in a foreign country. In many ways, then, the German prisoners' correspondence reverberated with similar feelings of longing and ties to home expressed by American prisoners of war in the letters they sent home across the Atlantic.

Besides the limitations on length, there were numerous restrictions placed on the prisoners' correspondence. They could not send maps, sketches, drawings or pictures of themselves. Letters had to be written in plain language with no hidden meaning. There could be no writing across or between the lines or crowding the lines, and absolutely no cyphers, codes, marks or shorthand. The content of the letters and postcards was to relate to family or business matters. Correspondence needed to be written in normal handwriting by the same person but could be written by the prisoner's company commander or another internee and countersigned by the person who wrote it.[98]

Letters could not contain quotations from books or include military information, and outgoing letters were not to be sealed. In their correspondence, the prisoners of war were prohibited from making objectionable comments; this could be the reason for the redaction of a few lines of text in the July 17, 1944 Werner Neubauer letter. Among the comments prohibited in prisoner of war letters were the following:

> *I can write only once a week.*
> *We are not permitted to register complaint.*
> *I can only write to close relatives.*
> *This is the seventh letter I have written you from here.*
> *You are not permitted to send me photographs.*[99]

As it pertained to incoming mail, prisoners of war could receive family photographs, but any photographs, pictures or drawings considered objectionable per army guidelines were forbidden. Packages were opened, inspected and censored in the presence of the prisoners and could not

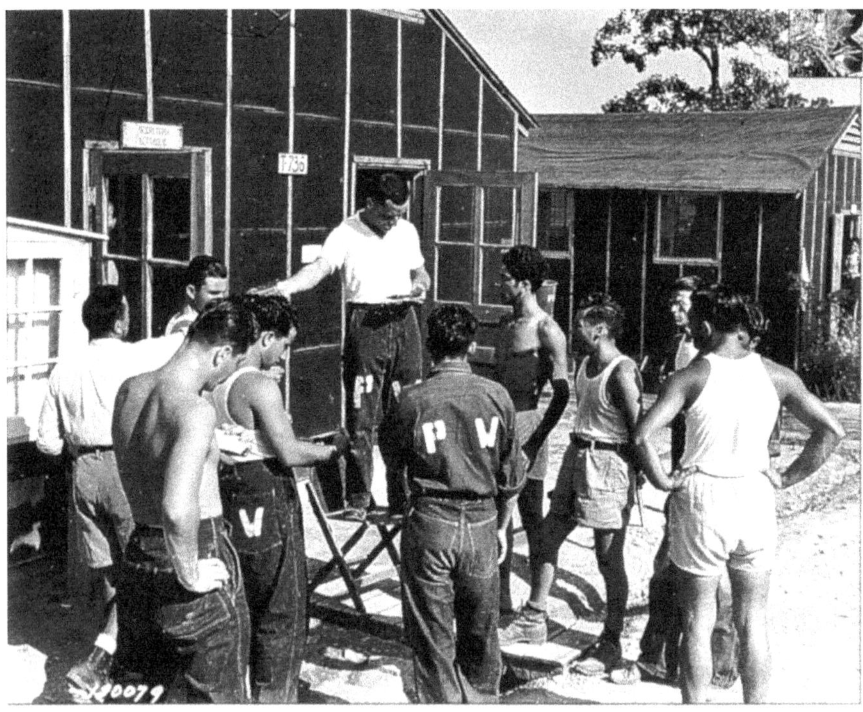

Italian prisoners of war at mail call at Camp Perry. *Courtesy of the Ottawa County Historical Museum at Camp Perry, Peggy Debien, curator.*

exceed four pounds unless prepaid.[100] The mail call was important to the prisoners of war, since it kept them in contact with their families and relatives back home.[101]

OBSERVATIONS

The prisoners of war were well aware of the censorship restrictions placed on their correspondence, as seen in the Werner Neubauer letter and the Werner Martick postcard. Given their stark feelings of isolation while in captivity, it seems likely that the prisoners of war did not want to jeopardize their ability to communicate back home, as it was their one welcome relief to receiving food and correspondence from loved ones and maintaining their ties to family and homeland.

7
CAMP LIFE

RELIGION

The religious needs of the Italian prisoners of war were being served each Sunday by a U.S. Army chaplain priest assisted by a local padre.[102] After the Italians left for the Erie Proving Ground and other branch camps, the German prisoners of war were served by two chaplains every Sunday. One of the Catholic priests spoke German, but the prisoners of war wanted a German chaplain who spoke German.[103] At a later date, a Protestant minister who spoke German was assigned to the camp. The main camp chapel, which was dedicated in 1943, was possibly used at times by the German prisoners of war.[104]

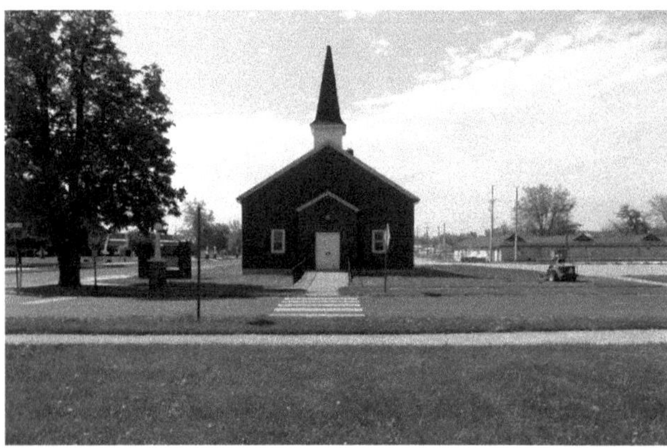

Chapel possibly used by German prisoners of war at Camp Perry. *Courtesy of the author's collection with approval of the Ohio National Guard and Camp Perry Joint Training Center.*

The December 15, 1945 edition of the *Der Aufbau* camp newspaper listed the times of the religious services.[105]

Lutheran		
Sunday, December 16 (3rd Advent)	8:30 a.m.	Regular service
	8:00 p.m.	Questions & answers
Wednesday, December 19	8:00 p.m.	Bible study
Catholic		
Sunday, December 16 (3rd Advent)	9:50 p.m.	Regular service
	7:00 p.m.	Prayer service
Thursday, December 20	8:00 p.m.	Prayer service
Saturday, December 22	7:30 p.m.	
Confession: Saturdays, before and after Mass		

Chart 10. List of Religious Services at Camp Perry. *Courtesy of New York Public Library, Der* Aufbau, *December 15,1945.*

RECREATION AND LEISURE TIME

The camp established two theaters—a stockade theater with a seating capacity of nine hundred and a smaller theater—that showed movies each week on 16-mm projectors. Volleyball and soccer equipment was provided that had been purchased from canteen profits and donations from local welfare agencies. The camp had one large recreation room equipped with furniture, table tennis facility, card tables and a floor table. When the camp first opened, the Italian prisoners of war established a sixty-four-piece orchestra, a sixty-voice choir and theater guilds that offered weekly entertainment.[106]

According to the February 27, 1944 Inspection Report by Dr. Benjamin Spiro of the Legation of Switzerland, entertainment for the prisoners was provided by organized theater groups, musical groups and weekly motion pictures in the nine-hundred-capacity theater.[107]

The inspection visits of January 23–24, 1945, by Captain Walter H. Rapp indicated that the camp had sufficient space for indoor and outdoor recreation.[108] There were two smaller fields, a well-equipped gymnasium, two movie theaters that showed a matinee and two evening movies each day, and two beer halls separate from the canteen, in addition to six pool tables and forty-five radios, as indicated in the February 13, 1945 Inspection Report of Dr. Rudolph Fischer of the Legation of Switzerland.[109]

When the Germans arrived and replaced the Italian prisoners of war at Camp Perry, they developed musical events like those listed in the October 6, 1945 edition of the *Der Aufbau* camp newspaper: (1) "Sunday, October 7—Camp radio will transmit at 4:45 p.m. the program"; (2) "Music for Sunday afternoon: 'Cheerful Dancing Melodies' by the Little Dancing Radio Orchestra"; and (3) "Sunday evening there will be in the new Movie House (Theater) a concert (records)—Something for Everyone!"[110] The December 6, 1945 edition of the newspaper listed the upcoming radio music on Sunday afternoon, December 9, featuring the orchestras of Xavier Cugat and Guy Lombardo, soprano singers Deanna Durbin and Dinah Shore and baritone Bing Crosby.[111] The December 15, 1945 edition of the camp newspaper announced a Christmas concert to be held the evening of December 16, showcasing the camp orchestra directed by Heinz Behmisch and Hans Hecker, both German prisoners of war. The concert featured the following program:[112]

> *1st Part*
> *Overture to "Rosamunde" by Franz Schubert*
> *Fantasy from "Hansel and Gretel" by Engelbert Humperdink*
> *"Nutcracker Suite" by Peter Tschaikowsky*
>
> *2nd Part*
> *Medley of the most famous movie and hit music from the time of our imprisonment:*
> *Soloists Hans Jahnke, harmonica*
> *Walter Fritz, trombone*
> *Announcers Fritz Bohnoff*
> *Konrad Fiend (MC at "Flimerkiste"* [Most likely, movies.]*)*

The Germans immersed themselves in the myriad movie options, including *Arrowsmith*, a Samuel Goldwyn film about the battle of medical science and starring Helen Hayes and Ronald Coleman; *The Great Victor Herbert*, a Paramount movie featuring Mary Martin, Allen Jones and Walter Conolly that depicted the life of an actress and actor who are friends of Victor Herbert; and the famous Irish American operetta and movie, *You Were Never Lovelier*, a love story set to music starring Fred Astaire and Rita Hayworth and put out by Columbia Pictures.[113]

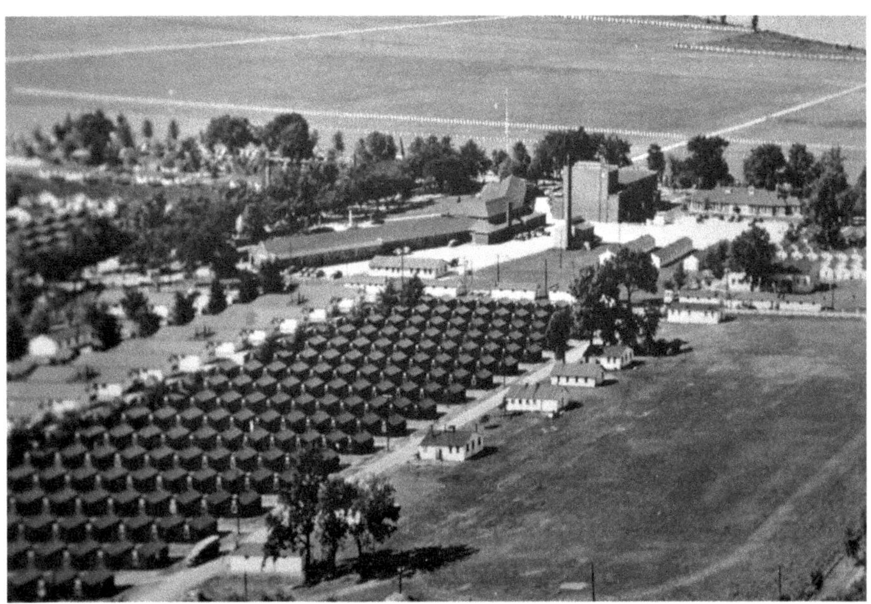

German hutments next to the athletic field at Camp Perry. *Courtesy of Steve Cooper, general manager and marketing manager of the Civilian Marksmanship Program at Camp Perry.*

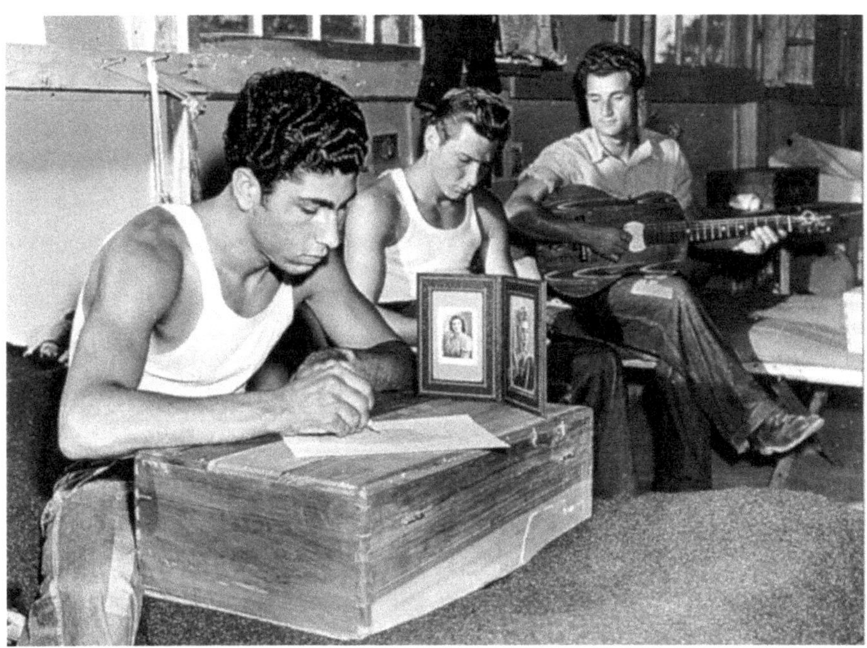

Italian prisoners at Camp Perry writing letters to families. *Courtesy of the Ottawa County Historical Museum, Peggy Debien, curator.*

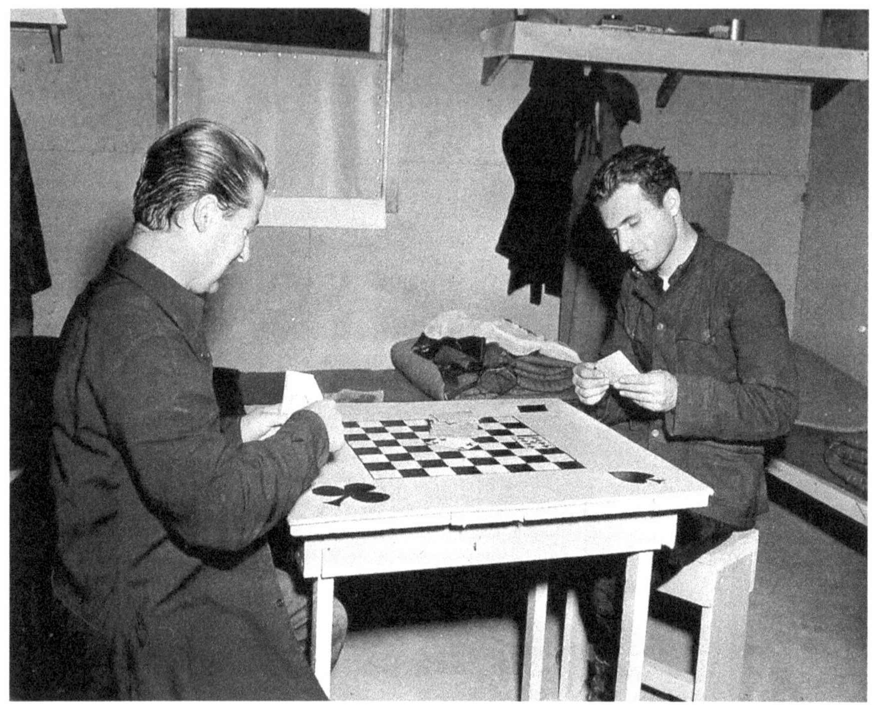

Italian prisoners of war at Camp Perry playing cards. *Courtesy of the Ottawa County Historical Museum, Peggy Debien, curator.*

In addition to cultural events, the *Der Aufbau* listed numerous sporting and gaming activities to round out the Germans' recreational pursuits that included soccer, table tennis and chess, in addition to an athletic field next to their hutments.[114]

During leisure time, the prisoners of war wrote letters home[115] and played cards[116] to break up the monotony and enjoyed table tennis, soccer and watching movies, whether in their native language or in English.

TRENCH ART BY ITALIAN PRISONERS OF WAR

The Camp Perry prisoners of war explored various kinds of artistic expression, including paintings and wood carvings, as seen in the accompanying photographs.[117] Trench art was a specialized form of art made behind a barbed-wire stockade that mirrored the effect of being in the trenches during

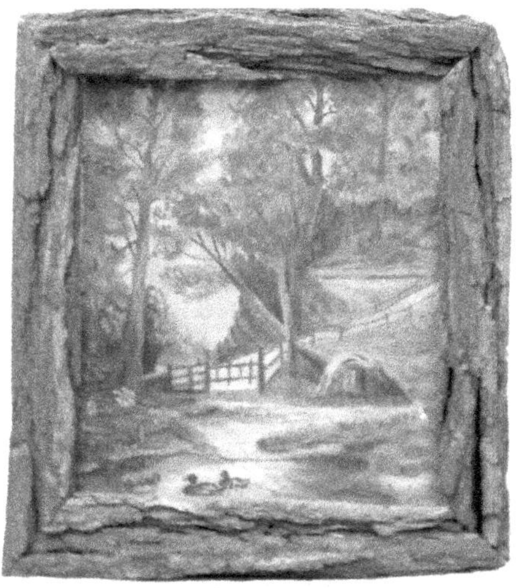

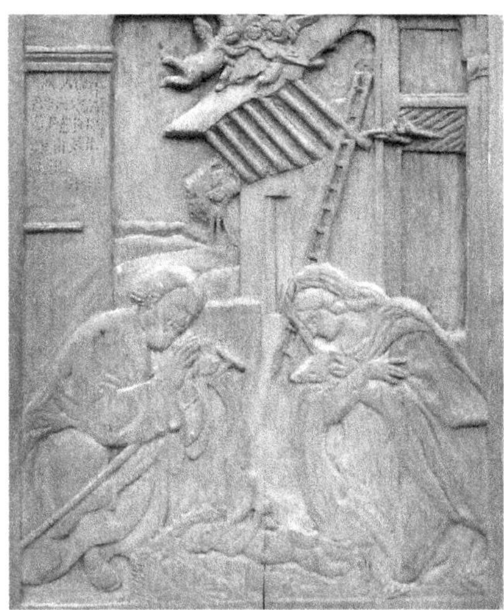

Left: Painting done by an Italian prisoner of war at Camp Perry. *Courtesy of the author's collection with approval of the Ottawa County Historical Museum.*

Right: Nativity scene carving done by Italian prisoner of war from scrap wood. *Courtesy of the author's collection.*

wartime. The painting of the tranquil setting must have reflected the feeling of an Italian prisoner of war when he put brush to canvas. The carving of the Nativity scene marked how a prisoner used only the materials available to him as a chance to channel his faith through his art and as a means to endure his confinement in a foreign land. Artistic expression allowed the prisoners of war an outlet to express their inner feelings while making their confinement more bearable.

CANTEEN

The camp canteen was a popular location, especially for the prisoners of war who had eight-hour workdays. The camp had two canteens and a barbershop, with equipment provided by canteen funds. Barbers were paid by the same funds, which meant they provided a free service to the prisoners of war. The canteens had display cases with rings and watches, and it was here where prisoners of war with coupon books could buy such items.[118] Each prisoner of war was allowed five cigarettes and one bottle

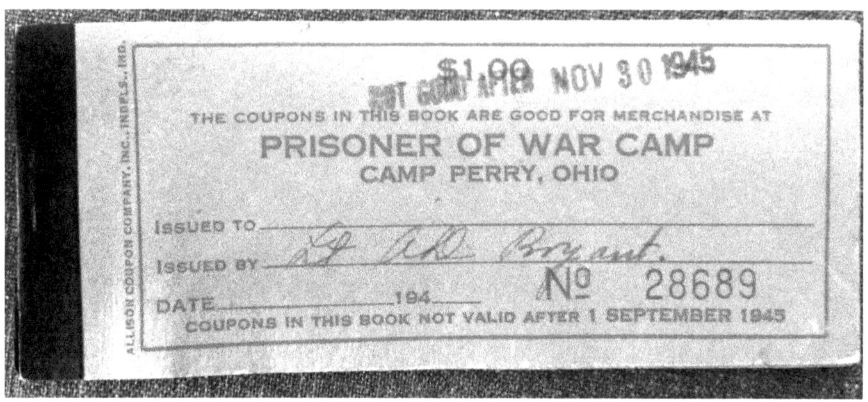

$1.00 NOT GOOD AFTER NOV 30 1945
THE COUPONS IN THIS BOOK ARE GOOD FOR MERCHANDISE AT
PRISONER OF WAR CAMP
CAMP PERRY, OHIO
ISSUED TO
ISSUED BY
DATE 194
No 28689
COUPONS IN THIS BOOK NOT VALID AFTER 1 SEPTEMBER 1945
ALLISON COUPON COMPANY, INC., INDPLS., IND.

Camp Perry coupon book. *Courtesy of Dave Frank.*

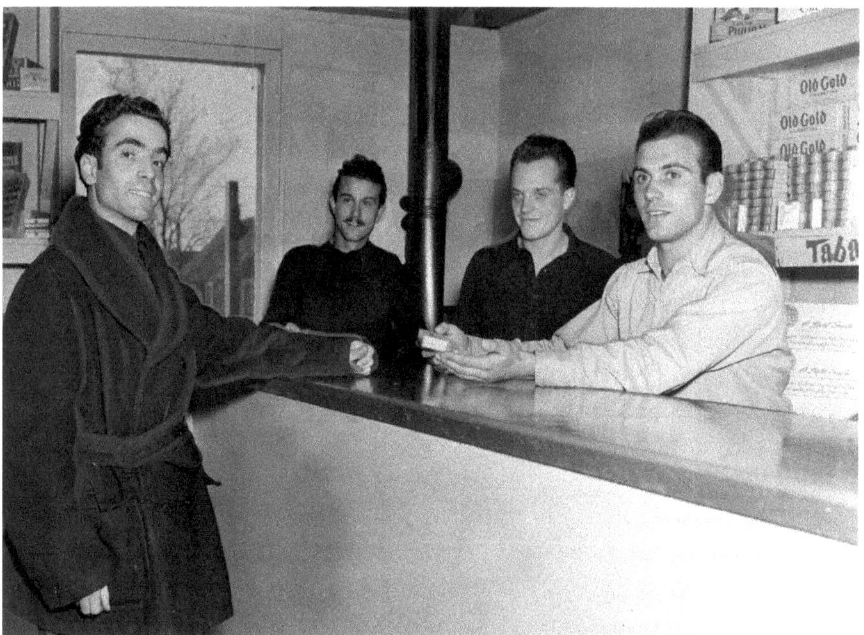

Italian prisoners of war buying cigarettes in a canteen at Camp Perry. *Courtesy of the Ottawa County Historical Museum, Peggy Debien, curator.*

of alcohol a day, but they could purchase additional cigarettes from the canteen,[119] making smoking essentially unlimited.[120] The prisoners of war enjoyed drinking soda pop in the canteen and the friendship of their fellow prisoners.[121]

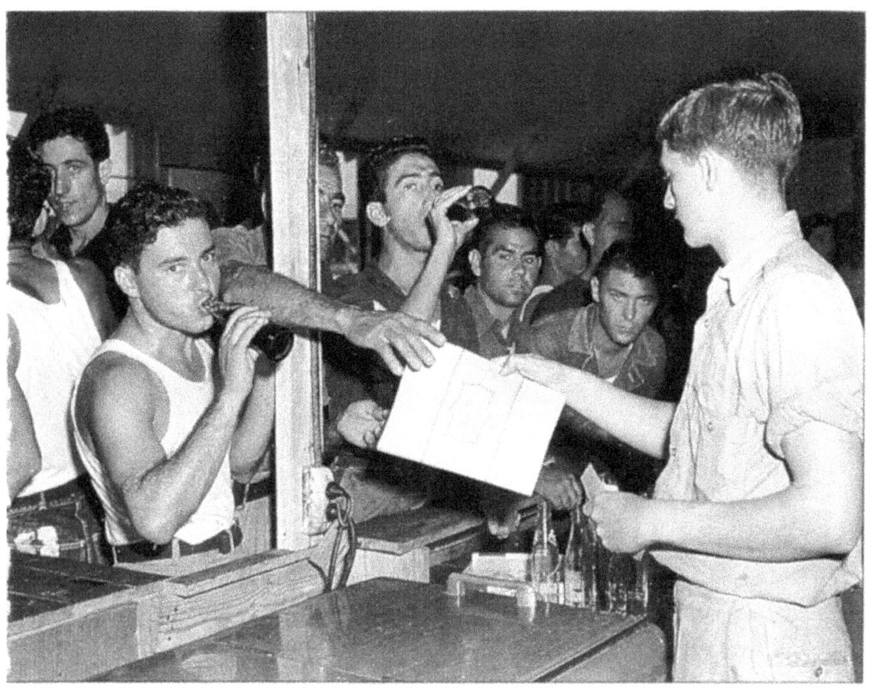

Italian prisoners of war drinking pop in a canteen at Camp Perry. *Courtesy of the Ottawa County Historical Museum, Peggy Debien, curator.*

Memorandum No. 9, issued on October 23, 1943, established the following operational guidelines for prisoner of war canteens at Camp Perry:[122]

> *Camp Perry POW Canteen Guidelines*
> *Hours*
>
> *Weekdays 5:00 PM to 9:00 PM*
> *Sunday 2:00 PM to 5:00 PM*
> *6:00 PM to 8:00 PM*
>
> *Profits*
>
> *(1) Profits from the canteen will be held in a Prisoner of War Canteen Fund and will be expended by the Camp Commander for the benefit of the prisoners as a whole to improve their health and well-being.*

PW Canteen Council

The Canteen Council will consist of the following:

Canteen Officer
Adjunct
Italian Camp Spokesman

Discipline

The canteen belongs to PW therefore each should make sure that he does his part to keep it clean and well disciplined.

No bottles will be removed from the canteen at any time. Bottles will not be left on the counter but will be placed in containers provided for that purpose.

Paper or refuse from candy, cigarettes, ice cream, etc., will not be thrown on the floor of the canteen or on the ground outside. All refuse will be placed in garbage cans.

A Change of Quarters will be on duty at the canteen at all times to guard against fire or loss of any merchandise.

OBSERVATIONS

The Camp Perry prisoners of war, who worked eight hours a day, five days a week, looked forward to the various recreational outlets granted them. The German prisoners' own camp newspaper, *Der Aufbau*, dedicated the majority of its pages to announcing the different recreational activities and programs at the camp. The newspaper even printed score updates of the camp teams to meet the Germans' high level of enthusiasm in the local sporting events. The most popular recreation facility for the Germans was the nine-hundred-seat movie theater that showed weekly movies. The canteen beer gardens that sold 3.2 beer were popular hotspots for relaxing and socializing with fellow prisoners of war. Given all these recreational outlets afforded to the Camp Perry prisoners, one can understand the concern raised by local newspapers that the camp was coddling a most hated enemy while brave men and women of Port Clinton were fighting against the Germans in Europe and, in some cases, making the ultimate sacrifice. A listing of fallen soldiers was recorded in the front-page notifications of the *Ottawa County News* and the *Port Clinton Herald and Republican* newspapers.

If Lieutenant Colonel McCormick Jr. had not established recreation opportunities for the prisoners of the war, he would have faced insurmountable discipline and violent upheavals at the base camp, especially with the arrival of the German prisoners of war.

8

PRISONER OF WAR PRIVILEGES

German prisoners of war were given privileges in a self-contained environment in their stockade, where they could operate bakeries, shoe repair shops, carpentry shops, mess halls, barbershops, canteens and the like. German prisoners most likely did not spend much time away from the stockade other than for working outside the base and branch camps.

Italian prisoners of war were another story, especially for those who joined the ISU and signed an agreement that obligated them to switch allegiance to the American cause of fighting the Axis powers. Like German prisoners of war, they ran their own mess halls and shops in the stockade, but because they were ISU members, those privileges extended beyond the base and branch camps. They could go on community inspections, attend social gatherings of local Italian American groups and write letters back home that exceeded the limit of what German and non-ISU prisoners of war could write.

The first inspection tour by ten Italian officers from Champ Perry, all of whom were ISU members, was on Sunday, June 2, 1944. They were escorted around Port Clinton and Marblehead peninsula, shown the Port Clinton Yacht Club, traveled along the lakefront to Catawba Island and then returned to Port Clinton to view the county and city buildings. Here they asked questions about the workings of the school and court systems, which provided the Italians with a better understanding of the American way of life. At the end of the day, the group toured Fremont, Ohio, where they attended church services and visited the Hayes Memorial and other historical places in the area.[123]

ISU members were given other limited privileges, such as seeing films with the theme of "Why we fight" in Italian, freedom of the post after duty hours in certain areas and permission to be in the main post exchange until 5:00 p.m. and a similar arrangement in their barracks area. Additional privileges included access to the post theater and visits from relatives after acceptance of a permission request.[124]

A visit to the Toledo Museum of Art was arranged for nine ISU members of the 323rd Italian Quartermaster Battalion of the U.S. Army from the Erie Proving Ground, one of whom remarked that the outside of the museum reminded him of Naples. The group also visited the civic center, zoological gardens and some residential areas of Toledo. Lieutenant Colonel Matteo Rossi, the ISU officer in command of the Italians under American officers, was impressed by the welcome they received during their tour of Toledo and hoped that this kind of cooperation would continue in the future. The ISU members were transported to the city by Miss Ruth Wainwright of Oak Harbor, a chauffeur at the Erie Proving Ground.[125]

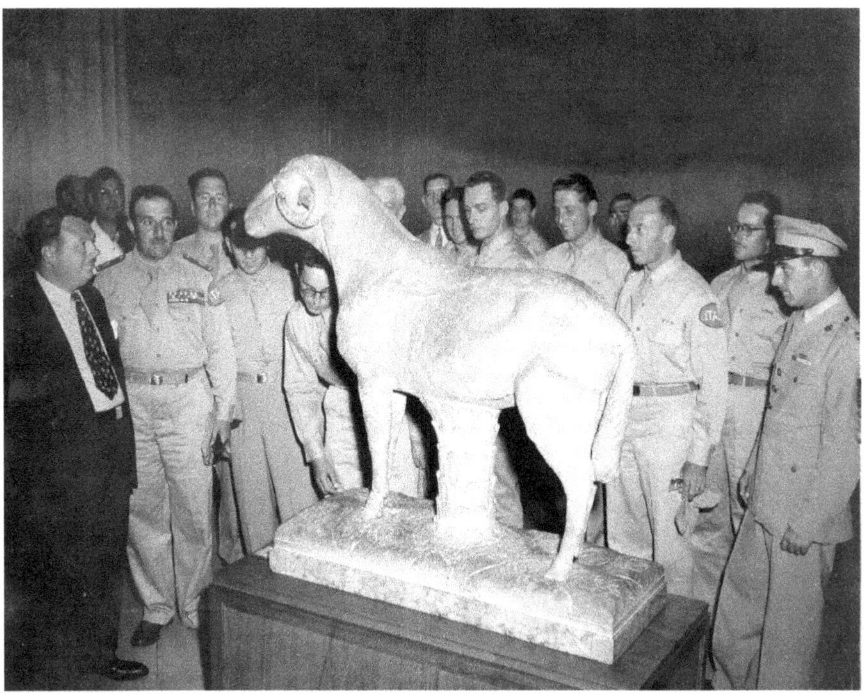

Italian prisoners of war from EPG viewing a Roman Ram at the Toledo Museum of Art. *Courtesy of the Ottawa County Historical Museum, Peggy Debien, curator.*

There was a public sentiment circulating in the United States that Sandusky, Ohio, warned the War Department that it was engaging in "pampering and hero worship" of former Italian prisoners of war. He was upset after a tour was scheduled of Sandusky and subsequently wired the War Department the following message:

> *The Congress has declared war against the Axis powers. What do you mean by parading around, finely outfitting, especially entertaining and hauling in Army trucks to Cleveland, Toledo and other northern Ohio cities the Italian prisoners from E.P.G. and calling them U.S. Army soldiers? Your officers advertising it as orientation for Italians. What do you mean by forcing these prisoners on the people as heroes, who killed our boys in Africa, Sicily, and Italy? I have witnessed no special honor treatment or entertainment by the War Department of the fathers and mothers whose sons are buried in North Africa, Sicily and Italy. Must the fathers and mothers of those who died in fighting these men, suffer such rot? It is discretion and mockery to those who gave their lives in North Africa, Sicily and Italy. I protest the pampering and hero worship of those who killed our boys. It is an insult to the fathers and mothers who gave their sons. The War Department is not authorized to use our boys as cannon fodder for the enemy and then make heroes the killers.*[126]

An insightful editorial followed the congressman's telegram, reading, in part: "Editorially speaking, this newspaper believes that Congressman Weichel must have been having a bad nightmare when he wrote the telegram. It greatly exaggerates the actual situation and overlooks the fact that the tour policy is 'insurance' against another war. As for 'hero worship,' one has to get further away from EPG and Camp Perry than Port Clinton is located before such an attitude can be detected—those Italians aren't suffering from 'hero worship' in this area!"[127] The pressure from Congressman Weichel, however, was enough to lead to the cancellation of the Sandusky tour.

Beginning in August 1944, a "Date Hut" was established at the Erie Proving Ground whereby guests were entertained by ISU members. A cafeteria, recreation hall and reception hall were available, plus rooms furnished as close to home as possible. There were three smaller rooms for entertaining one to two guests. Local girls could use these rooms if they had dates, and parents could use them to visit the girls and their dates. News of this social arrangement was covered in an August 18 newspaper article in the *Ottawa County News*: "A 'Date Hut' has been opened at

EPG Village, for the forty-six young ladies who make the Village their home."[128] The rules that applied to the use of the rooms were strict, patterned after what one would see in most colleges. The mayor of EPG Village, Bill Blose, was excited about the concept of the "Date Hut" and advocated expanding the program if it found favor among the village residents.[129] The *Toledo Blade* edition of October 5, 1944, ran the headline "Cradle of Postwar Democracy for Italians Being Carved at Erie Proving Ground—Captives of War Enjoying Freedom in Simplest Form." Under the headline, a picture showed young ladies and Italian prisoners of war with the caption: "Dancing with Visitors Is Continuous—Slow Waltzes Are the Vogue as the ISU Stag Line Waits."[130] It appears that the Date Hut concept was a big hit for EPG Village, both for the young ladies and the Italian prisoners of war.

Not only did the Erie Proving Ground have a Date Hut, but prisoners of war also had the opportunity each Sunday to be driven to the Sons of Liberty Club in Toledo, where they enjoyed beer, music, home-cooked food, meeting fellow Italians from the old country and dancing with girls from local Italian families.[131]

EDUCATION PROGRAMS

Education programs, known as "Intellectual Diversion," started to evolve at the base camp over time, the thrust of which revolved around changing the minds of the prisoners of war to embrace the tenets of American democracy. The February 27, 1944 Inspection Report indicated there were courses offered in English and that manual training and hobby and paint shops were being organized. The prisoners of war—at this time all of whom were Italian—had subscriptions to two American Italian-language papers; however, it was reported, "neither of which it is understood are particularly outstanding." The Italian prisoners also had access to 350 books in Italian.[132] The October 6 Inspection Report noted that several prisoners, probably German, would be registering for university courses designed to their interest.[133] The education program continued to expand at the base camp, as seen in the January 23–24, 1945 Inspection Report, which reported that Dean Carter of the University of Toledo committed to implementing an education program for which he would provide textbooks for the classes to be offered.[134] By the time the February 13 Inspection Report was released, the education program had increased to such a degree that there was interest in reviewing the atlas of the United States.[135]

The July 11, 1945 edition of the *Ottawa County News* featured a headline that read "TEACH ENGLISH TO GERMAN PW'S AT CAMP PERRY—Classes Being Conducted to Teach Language and American History to Prisoners." The article read as follows:

> *In line with the belief that better international relations can only come through understanding, classes in English language are now being conducted for German prisoners of war at Camp Perry and its branch camps throughout Ohio. Attendance is on a voluntary basis and classes are soon to be enlarged to include as high as sixty percent of the prisoners. In addition to English, classes have been set up in American History with a prelude In the study and understanding of the American Constitution, in the Social Sciences As pertains to the way they are practiced in western civilization, and in the economic geography of America. The education program is one based on simple truths which is something that, in part, has been missing in the German educational system during the past 12 years. Through this program, Army officials believe the German prisoner of war will come to realize the industrial might and indomitable spirit of the people of the United States of America. There are large numbers of German prisoners of war in the U.S. who will be repatriated someday, and upon their return to Germany will naturally have a part to play in the reformation Germany. Their opinions concerning America may determine, in a large measure, future relations between Germany and the United States. With this in mind, the German PWs, under the control of Camp Perry and its branch camps at Cleveland, Columbus, Bowling Green, Defiance, Marion, Cambridge are now afforded the opportunity to grasp a better understanding of America and its institutions. In this way, there will be created voluntary responses on the part of the German PWs which will encourage an attitude of respect on their part for American Institutions, traditions and ways of life and thought.*[136]

The *Der Aufbau* newspaper of December 15, 1945, noted the continuance of the five English-language classes—the oldest having started in October 1944 soon after the arrival of the German prisoners of war—but that all would be discontinued once Camp Perry is dissolved. The newspaper also indicated that about four hundred prisoners of war were enrolled in American history classes and that all of the students passed the final exam.

American history appeared to be the major course concentration of the camp. The newspaper provided notice that on December 17 there would be filmstrips with topics from the previous classes shown in the beer halls of the Second Battalion on Mondays, Thursdays and Fridays between 8:00 p.m. and 9:00 p.m. There would be time for discussion and "everyone is invited, also friends, who had participated in classes." The newspaper continued: "Special edition of the booklet 'Basic Features of American History' a special booklet covering eleven topics of History classes in its basic features, with maps and sketches is being published with the format equal to camp newspaper. The booklet is free of charge and can be ordered by everyone interested and there will be sufficient copies at the outlying camps."[137]

The number of men enrolled in American history classes at Camp Perry continued to increase, an indication that the camp was trying to reach a broader audience through the newspaper and tell the story of a free America before the prisoners of war would be repatriated to Germany. The American history courses were a subtle way of portraying the freedoms of the United States versus the dictatorship of the Nazi regime that eliminated the freedoms and human rights that at one time were prevalent throughout Germany.

As part of the Intellectual Diversion program, the camp showed films to the prisoners of war featuring American movie stars portraying the idyllic American life. Another part of the program showed films in the post theater about German atrocities filmed by newsreel cameras. The hardcore Nazis, however, viewed the films cynically as merely a continuation of the U.S. propaganda machine aimed at debunking the bill of goods sold by the Nazi regime.

OBSERVATIONS

The idea of granting privileges to prisoners of war housed in the United States generated a fear that the government was "coddling" the prisoners on home soil, a theme that resonated in the *Ottawa County News* and the *Port Clinton Herald and Republican* newspapers. Camp Perry officials would counter this claim by pointing out that the prisoners were held in strict confinement similar to any prison and that the prisoners were also filling a labor shortage in the area.

Toward the end of the war, the Intellectual Diversion program implemented by the base and branch camps included offerings in English and American history classes that afforded the prisoners of war the opportunity to gain a more comprehensive understanding of America and its institutions. The top priority was to instill in the minds of the German prisoners of war a respect for American institutions, traditions and ways of life and thought before being repatriated.

9

CAMP PERRY WORK PROGRAM

In preparation for the incoming Italian prisoner of war workforce, Major E.C. McCormick Jr., camp commander, issued the following memorandum on Labor of Internees, based on the provisions of the Geneva Convention of July 27, 1929, Treatment of the Prisoners of War:

> *1. "The labor of the bodied internees will be utilized according to their rank and aptitude. Non-commissioned officers will only be required to supervisory work, unless they expressly request a remunerative occupation." (Art. 27, Geneva Convention, 1929)*
>
> *2. "No Internee will be employed for which he is physically unfit." (Art. 29, Geneva Convention, 1929)*
>
> *3. Except in emergencies, the working day will not be longer than ten hours, but this limitation does not constitute a habitual ten-hour working day. "Every internee will be allowed a rest of twenty-four consecutive hours every week, preferably on Sunday." (Art. 30, Geneva Convention, 1929). In no event will the interval between successive rest days be longer than nine days.*
>
> *4. "Internees will not receive wages for work connected with the administration, management, and maintenance of the camp." (Article 34, Geneva Convention, 1929). Such unpaid labor will be termed "Class One" labor hereafter in this memorandum. "Internees utilized for other work shall be entitled to wages." (Art. 34, Geneva Convention, 1929). Such paid labor hereafter in this memorandum will be termed "Class Two" labor.*[138]

Class One labor at Camp Perry was focused on maintaining and repairing the barracks and all areas requiring maintenance, such as sanitary facilities and fencing. Company cooks, tailors, cobblers, barbers, clerks and any support workers in these areas were classified as Class One labor.

Class Two labor consisted of any farm and private industry work performed by the prisoner of war outside the camp stockade.

LABOR DEPLOYMENT

Camp Perry established a Class Two labor pay schedule for the prisoners of war that involved paying the prisoners 50 percent of their amount earned during the month in addition to a regular three dollars a month allowance; the balance of their percentage earnings was credited to a trust fund.[139] The accompanying chart extrapolates the pay schedule as a means of illustrating the variances in pay.

Days Worked	Total Work Allowance Due	Plus Regular Monthly Allowance	Total	Amount Paid PW	Amount Deposited
½	$.40	$3.00	$3.40	$3.00	$.40
1	.80	3.00	3.80	3.00	.80
26½	21.20	3.00	24.20	3.00	9.20
27	21.60	3.00	24.60	3.00	9.60

Table 2. Class Two Labor Pay Schedule. *Courtesy of NARA, Memorandum 240/3, January 4, 1944.*

The labor shortage in Northwest Ohio, and throughout Ohio as a whole, was acute in both farming and private industries. As a result, the War Department established Camp Perry as a main prisoner of war base camp for the state because it had an existing military facility that could readily be converted to housing prisoners of war. These prisoners were apportioned to area farms and private industries from Camp Perry and through the branch camps—which included General Hospital in Cambridge and Crile General Hospital in Parma—thus reaching a wider audience.

The War Department issued certificates of need for agricultural and industrial work, areas that had labor shortages, and the prisoners of war were thus able to fill these labor gaps. The local War Department agent in the Camp Perry region would expedite the certificate process during the peak harvest time of August through October. During this three-month period, a twelve-hour workday was authorized for the prisoners of war, which included four hours of travel time to and from Camp Perry, with the justification that these additional work hours would only be for three months out of the year.

Labor deployment at Camp Perry began when the more than one thousand Italian prisoners of war arrived in October 1943. The strategy was to split the labor between the military base, which consisted of unpaid prisoner labor, with contract labor from prisoners at area farms and private industries,[140] labor that was paid in accordance with the Class Two pay schedule. At the time, there was a particular manpower shortage in the tomato fields and fruit orchards, and the use of the prisoners of war helped fill this labor gap.

Prisoner of war labor to farmers and other eligible employers expanded after the second group of several hundred Italians arrived at Camp Perry on February 11, 1944.[141] A number of ISU members were then relocated to the Erie Proving Ground on May 12, where they were assigned to recondition and service artillery guns and to load and unload trucks.[142] The last group of ISU members at Camp Perry was transferred on November 3 to the Rossford Ordnance Depot, leaving the only remaining ISU members in the area at the Erie Proving Ground.[143]

The first group of several hundred German prisoners of war arrived at Camp Perry on June 2, 1944, and would be available for gardening and food processing that fall.[144] In June 1944, an expedited certificate of need for agricultural and industrial work was put to the test with 3,500 German prisoners of war called for to assist with food processing. The certificate was ready to be issued with the arrival of the second group of German prisoners on July 7, twenty-one days after the D-day invasion in Normandy, France.[145] On September 8, several hundred additional German prisoners of war captured in France arrived at Camp Perry and were added to the labor pool.[146] On January 19, 1945, the third group of German prisoners of war who had been captured in the Mediterranean and European theater of operations arrived at Camp Perry.[147] The final and fourth group of about 1,000 captured German navy prisoners from Camp McCain, Mississippi, arrived at Camp Perry on August 3, 1945, to assist with the labor shortage in Ohio and northern Indiana. Many of these prisoners were assigned to the various Camp Perry branch camps.[148] The Inspection Report of August 17 stated that there were 2,732 German prisoners of war at Camp Perry and 3,093 at its branch camps, totaling 5,825 German prisoners of war attached to Camp Perry as a whole.[149] This number did not include the Italian prisoners of war who were housed at the Erie Proving Ground and at the Rossford Ordnance Depot in Rossford, Ohio.

SAMPLE CONTRACTS

As the labor force and pages of associated contracts continued to expand at Camp Perry, McCormick, who had now become the camp's lieutenant colonel and commanding officer, issued a memorandum on October 13, 1944, to all contractors using Camp Perry's prisoners of war. His concern was that the full eight-hour workday was not being utilized because transportation was being included as part of the hours worked. McCormick made it clear that it was the responsibility of the contractor to provide adequate transportation and that transportation time was not to be counted as part of the eight-hour workday. He was also concerned that the prisoners of war were not receiving a one-hour lunch period or five-minute or fifteen-minute rest periods in the morning and afternoon, time that would not be compensated for by the contractor so long as the prisoners were working eight-hour shifts. Another concern was that there should not be more than twelve hours of elapsed time to and from the camp, which may have occurred in some cases and violated the laws of the Geneva Convention.[150]

Some examples of contracts and billings obtained from the Ottawa County Historical Museum include a labor contract for picking produce on the Engleback farm,[151] a billing statement for work performed between September 6 and 9, 1944,[152] and a billing statement for transportation costs for the work period between September 5 and October 1.[153] Although these contracts indicate the work was for picking produce and peaches, some prisoners of war likely also worked at the Engleback cannery.

The labor output from Camp Perry was very productive, as evidenced from the April 11, 1945 Labor Contract Details Report that showed the camp had eighty contracts in effect stretching from Toledo to Cleveland. These contracts involved a total of 965 prisoners of war who were involved in the labor force at farms and businesses, and some 96 guards who were required to watch over them at the eighty various locations. This same report indicated that 823 German prisoners of war were assigned to post duties out of the total number of 1,788 German prisoners who made up the external and post labor force.[154]

In comparing the Strength Report of January 14, 1944,[155] to the External Contract Detail Report, one finds an increase in Post and external labor support. The German prisoners of war had now become the labor force at Camp Perry after replacing the ISU members, who were moved to the Erie Proving Ground and Rossford Ordnance Depot.

PRISONER OF WAR CAMP
Camp Perry, Ohio

320.2/2 — 14 January 1944 (Date)

STRENGTH REPORT

	Co A	Co B	Co C	Co D	Total
Strength	250	250	250	265	1015
1. Company Overhead	16	17	15	16	64
2. PW Cp Overhead	11	2	5	5	23
2.A Company Duty	4	4	4	4	16
3. Sk in Hospital	1	4	4	7	16
4. Sk quarters	13	0	2	12	27
5. Confinement	0	0	1	0	1
6. Sk—no work	1	1	4	4	10
7. Sick Call	10	19	14	7	50
8. EPG Projects	88	111	131	74	404
9. Rosford Ord Projects	53	48	30	61	191
10. Industrial Contracts	0	6	0	8	14
11. Agricultural Contracts	5	0	0	0	5
12. Post Engr Projects	21	8	14	51	94
13. QM Projects	10	0	9	0	19
14. Cp Perry Projects	11	19	9	7	46
TOTAL	243	239	242	256	980
Not Working	7	11	8	9	35

PWCP Form No. 24

TABLE 3. Camp Perry POW Strength Report, January 14, 1944. *Courtesy of NARA, PWCP Form No. 24, January, 14, 1944.*

LABOR FORCE GOING HOME

Although German prisoners of war were still arriving at Camp Perry as of August 1945, a letter dated April 17, 1945, from M.G. Carpenter, Captain, CM.P. Work Project Officer, Sixth Service Command to Ralph Strong, National Director Region #5, War Manpower Commission, Cleveland, Ohio, stated the command had received notification from the Provost Marshal General's Office that a decision had been made by the War Department to discontinue the shipment of prisoners of war to the United States on V-E day. The letter went on to say that any shipment of prisoners of war that had already commenced would be completed and to not be alarmed, as the letter was merely a matter of information. Concern over the loss of the prisoners of war for meeting the labor shortage on farms and local industries was raised in an April 20 letter from E.L. Keenan, regional director, to the War Manpower Commission in Washington, D.C.:

> *We strongly urge your office to take the necessary actions with the top Army Policy makers to ensure that promises made and relied upon by so many employers are kept. Unless we have favorable prompt assurance that the Army will deliver the workers promised we do not feel we can avert a series food shortage in Ohio and Michigan during the peak food processing season. If we have a prolonged period of mass unemployment (which we do not anticipate) it is true that we might get those food processing needs met by referral of laid-off industrial workers. In the meantime, however, we would undoubtedly have considerable crop loss and food spoilage.*[156]

It is evident that the prisoners of war were considered the backbone of the labor force that supported agricultural employers, who had locked in this support through the labor contracts. This securing of labor was especially important during the prime cultivation and harvesting seasons, as is seen in the schedules agreed upon with the area Works Projects Coordinator.

The correspondence of April 1945 portended the gradual sending home of the prisoners of war from Camp Perry. A *Toledo Times* headline on September 18, 1945, read, "Last PWs Leave Toledo Industries."[157]

OBSERVATIONS

The dependence on prisoner of war manpower to meet the labor shortages in area farms and private industries was crucial during harvest time and for supporting the manufacturing industry that worked to further the war effort, especially at the Erie Proving Ground and Marion and Rossford Ordnance Depots.

During the week of February 4, 1946, some 1,400 German prisoners of war were sent to ports of embarkation. The remaining 600 prisoners were shipped home the week of February 11, 1946, marking the closure of Camp Perry as an army post.[158] Allowing the German prisoners to stay until February 1946 provided enough time for farmers to harvest their crops, canneries to complete their food processing and industries to make labor adjustments, as the GIs who came home returned to the labor market.

10
CAMP PERRY'S BRANCH CAMPS

In the July 28, 1944 *Ottawa County News*, a headline read, "1500 Prisoners Slated to Work at Side Camps (Perry to Operate Ag. Camps at Defiance, Celina and Bowling)." According to the article, the branch camps were established to alleviate the critical agriculture labor shortage in Northwest Ohio, as announced by Colonel Harold P. Woosley, post commanding officer. These branch camps would be home to about 1,500 German prisoners of war.[159]

Prisoners at Camp Perry and its branch camps who worked outside the camps had to be certified by the War Manpower Commission that their work was needed. A prisoner was paid the prevailing local rate, which went to the U.S. Treasury, with the prisoner receiving eighty cents a day in canteen checks, or ten cents a day if he was not working.

This chapter will delineate the three side camps mentioned in the newspaper article and also provide information about the following camps and other institutions associated with Camp Perry: Wilmington POW Camp, Crile General Hospital, Fletcher General Hospital, Columbus ASF Depot, Thomas A. Scott POW Camp, Marion Engineer Depot, Scioto Ordnance Plant and Rossford Ordnance Depot.

DEFIANCE POW CAMP

A *Toledo Blade* article of September 26, 1944, entitled "Where Is Our Lather? Nazi PWs Getting Fat on GI Chow, Medical Officer Says" details the Defiance, Celina and Bowling Green POW branch camps. The Defiance, Ohio camp was housed in an old Civilian Conservation Corps (CCC) camp where the men were permitted to wear their army insignias and medals and were allowed to use radios free of shortwave attachments.[160] The newspaper reporter apparently even saw several small Nazi swastika flags hanging over the beds in the barracks.

The 425 German prisoners of war assigned to the Defiance camp consisted of 8 noncommissioned officers, 4 sanitary personnel, 1 chaplain and 412 soldiers brought in to assist with the harvesting of the tomato crops and to work in other private industries in the area. The camp was set up in old CCC buildings that accommodated five barracks heated by coal and housing 54 men. An additional fifty tents were also heated by coal and housed 3 to 4 men in each tent. The facility had a kitchen and mess hall, a recreation center with canteen and one building containing showers and dressing rooms, which made it possible to keep the camp open year-round if prisoner labor was needed. The U.S. Army soldiers guarding the prisoners of war were housed in tents and maintained the fence line around the camp.[161] Ironically, Italian prisoners who were transferred into a voluntary engineer service unit did the construction work to prepare the camp, which limited the cost to only $750.

There was no library at the camp, and educational programs were limited to specially designed university courses offered to several of the prisoners. Recreation opportunities were also limited to some sporting equipment, one athletic field, a few games, one piano and a radio. Religious services were conducted by a Catholic chaplain and a Protestant minister every Sunday.[162]

Prisoners were not only employed in farm and agricultural work but also repaired automobiles, transported food products and worked in sawmills and at the military depot painting cars and chopping wood. It was estimated that $50,000 to $60,000 in payments from prisoner of war labor during the summer season represented a profit to the U.S. Treasury.[163]

Because the camp was open year-round, it was able to enter into twelve labor contracts with local businesses and thus increased its payments to the U.S. Treasury. The Time Schedule for Active Work Projects—April 9, 1945 depicts the daily work schedule for the twelve labor contracts.[164]

Project	PW	Leave Camp	Start Work	Lunch Hour	Quit Work	Return to Camp
St. Marys Packing Co.	14	0700	0830	1200–1230	1700	1815
Defiance Milk Products	5	0750	0800	1130–1230	1700	1710
Smith Foundry/ Mach. Co.	5	0730	0900	1130–1230	1700	1830
C.H. Black Co.	5	0700	0830	1300–1400	1700	1830
Timmerman Sales Co.	10	0700	0830	1130–1230	1700	1830
Republic Creosoting Co.	10	0700	0900	1130–1200	1730	1830
Schulien & Sons Foundry	6	0700	0830	1300–1330	1730	1830
Bryan Handle Co.	10	0800	0900	1230–1300	1730	1830
Delphos Machine Co.	10	0700	0800	1200–1230	1630	1730
Schock/Mosier Laundry Co.	7	0700	0830	1200–1230	1700	1830
Baker/Schindler Contracting Co.	5	0715	0730	1130–1230	1630	1645
Pet Milk Co.	10	0745	0900	Unavailable	1700	1815
Total Prisoners of War	97					

TABLE 4. Defiance POW Camp, Active Work Projects. *Courtesy of NARA, Other Inspection Reports-Perry (Defiance), April 9, 1945.*

The table indicates that the work time at the Defiance POW Camp varied between seven and eight hours, with a norm of eight hours. Transportation to and from the camp, however, added another two to three hours onto the workday. Some of the more strenuous worksites, such as Schulien & Sons

Foundry and Delphos Machine Company, provided only half-hour lunches for an eight-hour shift, and when the two to three hours of travel time was factored in, this resulted in a rather laborious workday.

Randy Buchman, city historian at the Andrew L. Tuttle Memorial Museum in Defiance, said this about his encounter with the German prisoners of war:

> *I was a teenage boy during World War II. At age 16, I was hired by a shipping company. This company shipped guns and ammunition to the U.S. Army. My job was to pound nails into the shipping crates. The lumber was unloaded by German prisoners of war. They could not nail crates but could unload the lumber according to the Geneva Convention Regulations on treatment and use of POW's.*[165]

Mr. Buchman's story reinforces the fear at the time of the German prisoners' ability to cause problems, as compared to the nonthreatening ISU members who had access to hammers and other tools.

CELINA POW CAMP

The Celina POW Camp was located on a 4-H camp of thirteen acres on the northwest corner of manmade Grand Lake St. Marys, Harbor Point outside of Celina, Ohio. Some 294 German prisoners of war arrived at the camp on July 4, 1944, consisting of 1 noncommissioned officer, 2 sanitary personnel, and 291 privates between the ages of seventeen and eighteen. The Celina POW Camp closed in mid-October 1944 after the tomato harvesting season was over, when the prisoners of war were returned to Camp Perry.[166]

The camp was surrounded by a high fence and guard towers. Four small houses served as the canteen, administrative office, chapel and store, while a large barrack served as the kitchen and mess hall. Some ninety-eight tents housed three men each and provided a wash basin, while a separate building was used as a showering facility and latrine. Part of this building was reserved for use by the seventy American soldiers and officers who slept in cabins at the camp. An infirmary provided light and moderate care by a visiting doctor each day, while severe cases were transferred to the base hospital at Camp Perry.[167]

The Celina POW Camp had a small library of fifty books focusing on American history, but there was no organized study program, due to the prisoners' demanding work schedules. In the leisure time that they did have, the prisoners enjoyed playing Ping-Pong; listening to the radio; reading local newspapers; swimming in the lake; and playing football, softball and baseball on the large athletic field. Four to five prisoners of war even formed a small orchestra that played on Sundays. Religious services for Catholics and Protestants were conducted by American chaplains.[168]

The Inspection Report of October 5, 1944, indicates that 120 prisoners were working at one of three canning companies: Beckman and Gast Canning Company of St. Henry; Sharp Canning Company in Rockford and Ohio City; and Crampton Canneries, which later became Stokely, in Celina and Mendon.[169] The report also notes that another fifty men were picking tomatoes, and a third group of men was working at a tile factory.

The citizens of Celina were initially afraid of the German prisoners of war coming to Celina and had thoughts of leaving town, according to the article "From Burial Ground to Camp for War Prisoners" from the January 17, 1974 edition of the *Daily Standard*. The article reports, "The homes of some of the people who were involved with the prisoners were bombed and their lives were threatened, but apparently, no one was ever injured."[170] The negative feelings toward the German prisoners continued throughout the time they were housed at the prisoner of war camp.

The Celina POW Camp farmers used their own trucks and automobiles to pick up their allocated prisoners of war and outfitted their trucks with benches lining the inside backs, according to a *Toledo Blade* article of September 26, 1944. An armed American guard sat upfront in the truck with the driver, leaving the back of the truck unguarded. The reporter observed a scene burned into the soft wood by a prisoner of war that depicted a German soldier against a skyscraper and the prisoners in the United States. A revolving globe separated him from a girl—perhaps his wife—reading a letter in a small parlor. Underneath the globe was inscribed, "We'll meet each other again at home."[171]

An interesting story appeared in the January 17, 1974 edition of the *Daily Standard,* Celina's local newspaper. The article, "From Burial Ground to Camp for Prisoners," reports that an outbreak of syphilis occurred among twelve of the guards at the prisoner of war camp. The article went on to say: "It was rumored that a couple of spinsters in Edgewater Park supplied the guards of the camp with all the sexual pleasures they desired. This could have been a major reason for the spreading the disease"[172] There certainly was not any boredom for the camp guards.

BOWLING GREEN POW CAMP

The Ohio Agricultural Extension Service entered into a lease with the City of Bowling Green from April 1, 1945, to December 31, 1945, to erect a temporary prisoner of war camp on twenty-two acres of land located near the city's sewage treatment plan. The lease payment for the site was $20 per acre and $440 for the term of the lease.[173]

The camp was established to harvest the local tomato crop and process the tomatoes in the local canneries, where prisoners of war worked eight to nine hours per day and night shifts even on Sundays. The Bowling Green POW Camp housed 404 German prisoners, including 7 noncommissioned officers, 2 sanitary personnel and 395 soldiers, which later increased to more than 600 men. The camp was made up of only tents and had a canteen, exchange, kitchen with moveable stoves and infirmary with prisoners eating in an open-air seating arrangement. Because it was designed as a short-term camp, there was no organized study program.[174]

Recreational opportunities were minimal, with only three games of checkers, local newspapers and a large field for playing football. A doctor visited the camp infirmary every morning, and the very ill patients were sent back to the hospital at Camp Perry. A Protestant chaplain held services every Sunday; for some reason, there was no Catholic priest available for the prisoners. The prisoners of war were not satisfied with the recreational opportunities and inadequate number of latrines, showers and wash basins.[175] The camp was unoccupied on November 16, 1945, in satisfactory condition and returned to the City of Bowling Green in a signed agreement with the Ohio Agricultural Extension Service on November 27, 1945.[176]

WILMINGTON POW CAMP

Camp Wilmington was formed in concert with the Clinton County Rural Policy Group, a consortium of twenty-three farm groups that in the fall of 1945 faced an agricultural emergency. The group formulated a resolution that outlined their concerns and the need for prisoners of war to address the area labor shortage due to the war. The policy group passed a resolution stipulating that corn was to be the feed base for hogs and cattle going to market as pork and beef; however, because of the work shortage, there was no labor available to de-tassel the corn. The resolution went on to stipulate that Clinton County, Ohio, plant 200,000 acres of hybrid field corn to be used as hog feed that would produce 120 million pounds of pork, and for the canning industry to produce 7 million No. 2 cans of processed foods. By passing the resolution, the policy group signaled to the War Department the critical labor need in the Clinton County, Ohio region.[177]

A temporary camp was constructed mainly of tents for housing 250 German prisoners of war with 50 American soldiers.[178] The tent camp opened on July 23, 1945, on property owned by Hubert A. Barrett. The prisoners of war worked on six different farms spanning the property, fulfilling the need for harvesting the corn. At the end of the harvest, on October 13, the camp was closed, and the prisoners of war were relocated to Camp Perry.[179] The photo shows some German prisoners on break while working in the fields.[180]

Several area residents detailed their experiences during the time the prisoners of war were in Clinton County. Barbara Bay relates that the Wilmington prisoners of war worked to de-tassel the corn on her father's farm. When Barbara was home from college during the summer, one day when her father was busy, she went to pick up the prisoners of war in the family truck for their workday. Being only about sixteen years old, she was stopped by the highway patrol and told never again to pick up prisoners by herself. Bob German, who lived on his family farm, says that the German prisoners of war would third the corn by hand, giving room for the corn

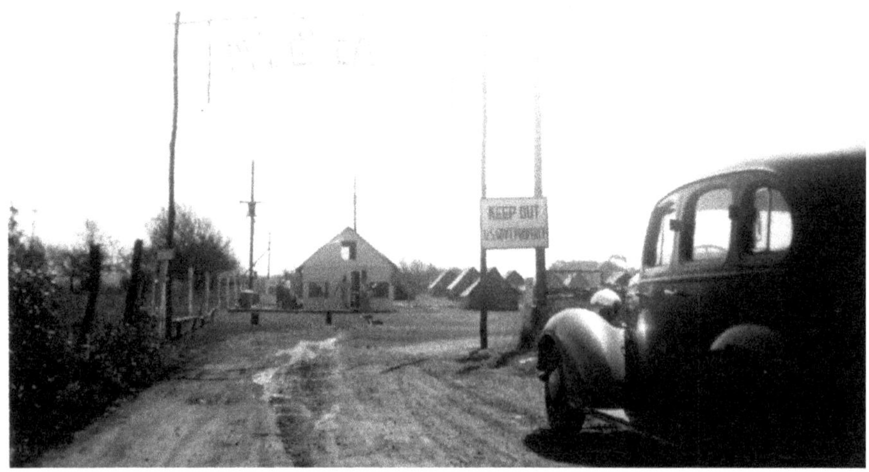

Wilmington, Ohio prisoner of war camp entrance. *Courtesy of the Clinton County Historical Center, Kay Fisher, director.*

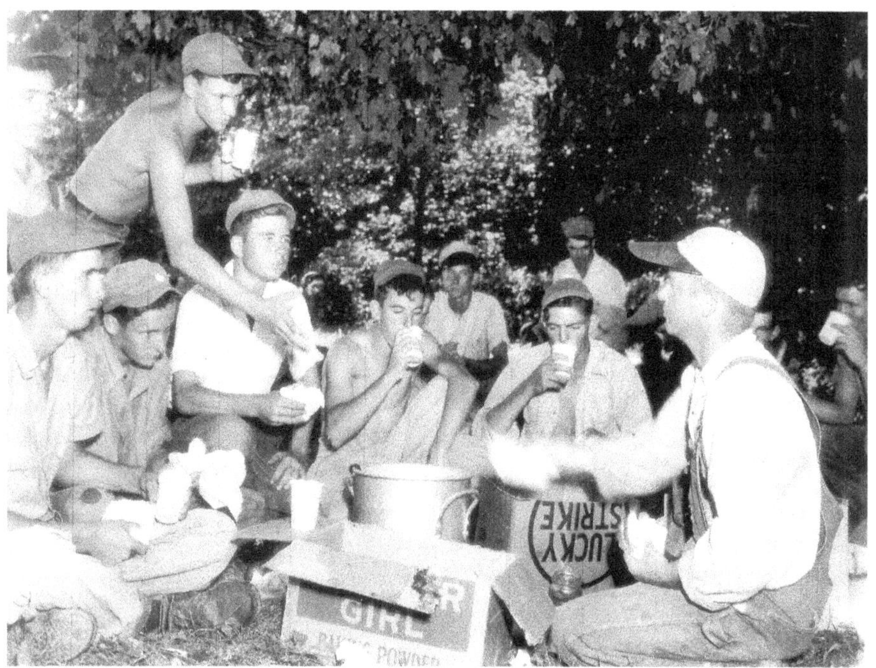

German prisoners of war at Camp Wilmington, Ohio. *Courtesy of the Clinton County Historical Center, Kay Fisher, director.*

binder to pick the remainder of the corn. The prisoners of war would then hand-bind the shocks around the base of the corn stocks. Ted Vandervort recalls his father owning a canning company and the German prisoners of war working side by side with the civilian women, whose husbands and sons were fighting overseas.[181]

The Wilmington POW Camp is a prime example of how prisoners of war housed in the United States were essential in meeting the labor needs and fulfilling the harvesting of a crop that helped put food on the tables across America.

Crile General Hospital

The Crile General Hospital was dedicated on April 21, 1944, and treated more than 15,000 wounded soldiers during World War II. The hospital map[182] shows it spanning 153 acres with close to 100 buildings. The facility was named after Dr. George W. Crile, a brigadier general in the U.S. Army during World War I, renowned surgeon and founder of the Cleveland Clinic Foundation. Today, the site is home to the Western Campus of the Cuyahoga Community College, the buildings of which were constructed to resemble those of the World War II Crile General Hospital.

The 245 German prisoners of war (consisting of 1 noncommissioned officer and 244 privates) who arrived on December 20, 1944, were divided into the work details of the hospital group and post-engineering group. A schedule of work dated April 3, 1945, indicates that the hospital group, comprised of 73 prisoners, was responsible for the mess halls, post laundry, sales commissary and quartermaster, and medical cleanup, which included window washing and floor cleaning. The post-engineering group, consisting of 173 prisoners, was responsible for the majority of the hospital maintenance, including, among other things, overseeing carpentry, working in the tool room, ditch digging, painting, landscaping, trash detail, electrical, plumbing, working in the coal pile and manning the incinerator.[183] The German prisoners of war lived in primitive barracks that met only their basic needs.[184]

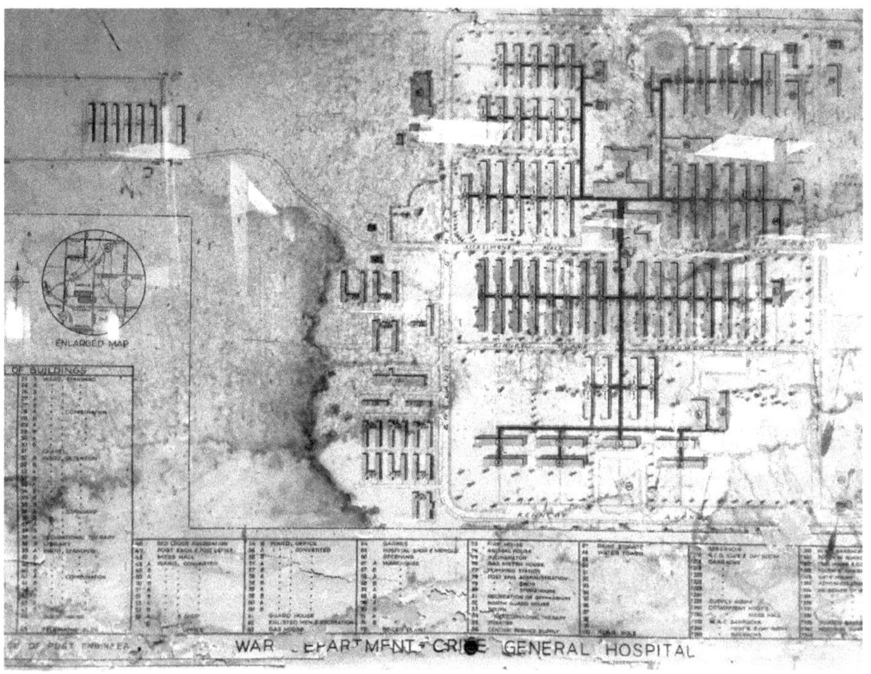

War Department map of Crile General Hospital. *Courtesy of the Crile Archive Center for History Education, James Banks, director.*

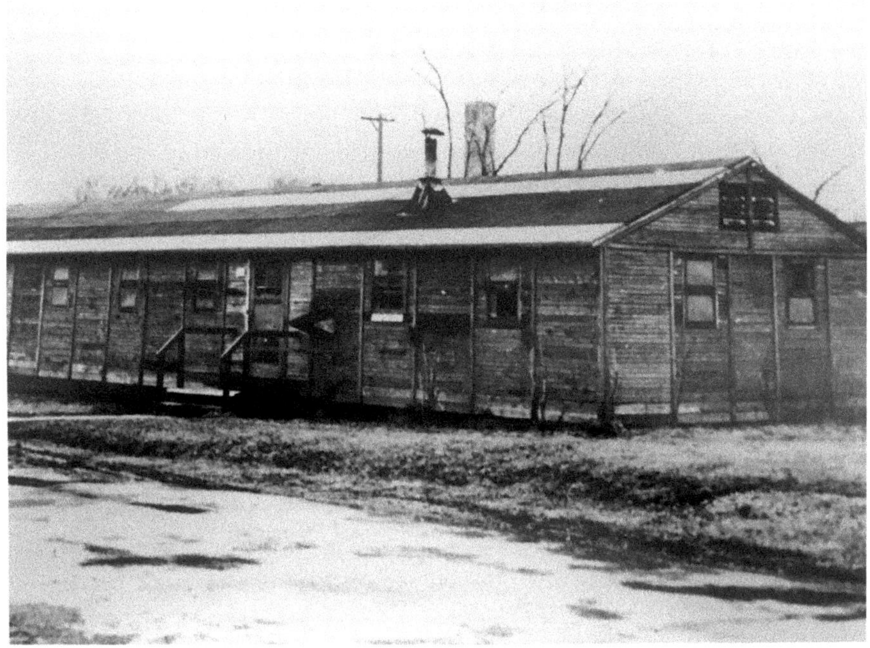

German prisoner of war barracks at Crile General Hospital. *Courtesy of the Crile Archive Center for History Education, James Banks, director.*

On January 19, 1945, a hospital guard shot and killed a German prisoner who had threatened him. The guard lost his balance on the icy ground and was rushed by the prisoner he shot. The guard went through a court-martial proceeding and was found not guilty.

Numerous newspaper articles across the United States mentioned how much better the prisoners of war were eating than civilians. A rationing point system was in effect during World War II for meats and canned goods, and it was opined by the Cleveland newspapers that the points for the prisoners of war at Crile General Hospital exceeded those of Cleveland residents, and thus they concluded that the prisoners had greater access to food than Cleveland families.

The 245 German prisoners of war at the Crile General Hospital filled a labor gap and contributed to the operation of the hospital, which specialized in orthopedic surgery and the rehabilitation of close to 15,000 wounded soldiers. In early 1946, the German prisoners of war left the hospital and were repatriated back to Germany.

FLETCHER GENERAL HOSPITAL

The Fletcher General Hospital grounds was located two and a half miles from Cambridge, Ohio, and covered 255 acres.[185] The hospital's 168 buildings had a capacity of two thousand beds by the end of the war. The facility opened on March 18, 1943, for general medicine. Combined with its specialty care in orthopedic medicine, it ended up receiving more than 17,000 wounded soldiers during World War II. The hospital was named after Lieutenant Colonel John Pierpont Fletcher, a career Army Medical Corps officer.[186]

The 191 German prisoners of war who arrived at the hospital in January 1945 were housed in barracks on-site. An April 4, 1945 work detail reported that for the month of January 1945 the prisoners of war worked a total of 2,592 man-days that included the following: (1) 194 Company and unpaid Stockade; (2) 206 Company and Stockade paid; (3) 42 PW canteen; (4) 1,828 outside camp work; and (5) 322 rest days. [187] It is evident that the German prisoners of war were major contributors to labor needs both inside and outside the Fletcher General Hospital.

The prisoner of war buildings included a mess hall, recreation facility and three structures for living quarters. A shoe repair shop was part of the salvage area and was operated by four prisoners who repaired an average of five hundred pairs of shoes per month. The typewriter and machine repair shop was also staffed by the prisoners of war and reportedly provided a major savings to the hospital.[188]

The hospital maintained a record of how many prisoners were working, including the camp commander's weekly report to his superiors. An example of the hospital's weekly report is seen in one from January 11, 1946.[189] The army used a "man-day" to account for work hours performed. If three men each worked only one day a week, it was reported as three man-days, which holds true if only one man worked all three days.

The January 31, 1946 Prisoner of War Labor Report outlines the job areas, with a total 1,828 man-days worked in the hospital, in addition to 442 man-days worked to maintain the stockade and canteen for a total of 2,270 man-days of work. When the credit for 322 man-days of rest—which normally occurred on Sundays—and 20 man-days for temporary medical reasons are factored in, the report culminates in a grand total of 2,612 man-days. The army recording man-days in its reports rather than the number of prisoners who were actually working at the hospital indicates that the army was predominantly interested in

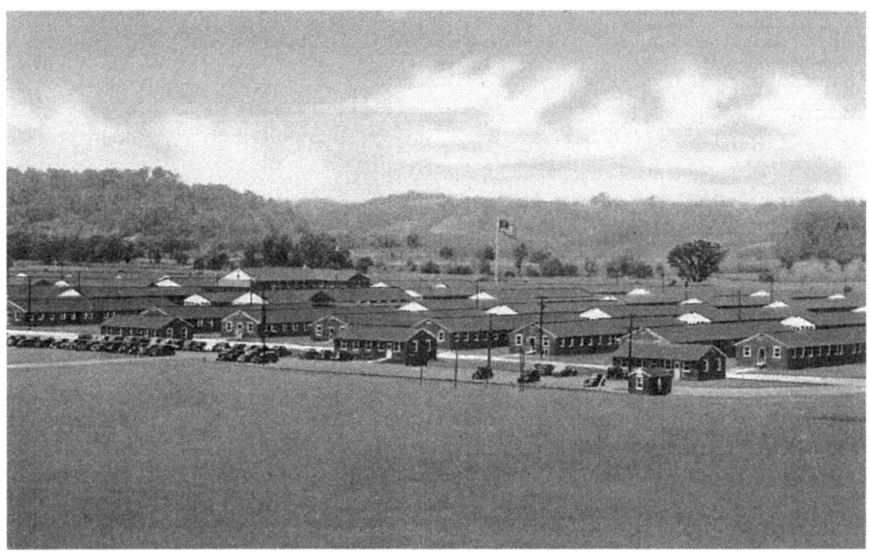

Fletcher General Hospital. *Courtesy of the author's collection.*

the labor produced and not the number of prisoners of war who worked at the hospital.

The number of incoming patients from European and Asiatic theaters peaked in 1945, with 3,117 patients on August 7, declining to an ending total of 1,849 patients on December 31. Declassified records show that there were 2,442 operations and 2,762 casts applied in 1945. It was reported that 165 trains were used to bring the wounded to the hospital. Overall, more than 80 percent of the patients returned to active service.[190]

The hospital provided numerous forms of entertainment for the wounded soldiers and army personnel. Big band leaders Tommy Dorsey and Gene Krupa, along with Sammy Kaye and his orchestra, performed for the patients. Actor Boris Karloff and child star Peggy Ann Garner—who had just filmed *A Tree Grows in Brooklyn*—also entertained the patients, who were shown movies for free at the on-site theater.[191]

The main focus of the hospital became orthopedic rehabilitation and the treatment of battle fatigue and shell shock. To facilitate this work, there were more than fourteen hundred civilian and military personnel, in addition to the prisoner of war labor, who made up the workforce at the hospital. The hospital closed its doors on March 31, 1946, later reopening as Cambridge State Hospital.

COLUMBUS ASF DEPOT

Situated on more than 500 acres, the Columbus, Ohio Army Service Forces Depot was the largest military supply center in the world. The depot's workforce of more than 10,000 civilians and 415 prisoners of war supported U.S. troops overseas during World War II.[192] The accompanying photo shows the depot grounds.[193]

The 415 prisoners of war consisted of 1 noncommissioned officer and 414 privates assigned to work in such areas as general cleanup and construction. The majority of prisoners were assigned to railroad repair, assembly line, carpentry shop, storage work, lumber unloading and cleaning, salvage box operations and mechanical details as seen in the Daily Labor Report Summary of April 4, 1945.[194] It is evident that the prisoners of war at the Columbus Depot were key contributors to the warehouse operations, in the expediting of key supplies and materials overseas in support of U.S. troops and allies.[195]

PW Branch Camp, Columbus, Ohio
Army Service Forces Depot
Daily Labor Report Summary
April 4, 1945

1. Strength
   a. Non-commissioned Officers ____ 1
   b. Privates ____ 414
   Total 415

2. Not Available for Work
   a. Hospitalization ____ 1
   b. Sick call, dental appointment ____ 18
   c. Essential unpaid labor (company duty) ____ 15
   Total 34

3. PW Camp Labor (paid)
   a. Overhead (interpreters, clerks, cooks, etc.) ____ 16
   b. Canteen & barber shop ____ 3
   c. Stockade Adm. (Spokesmen, infirmary aides, etc.) ____ 6
   d. Functions related to the occupancy of the camp ____ 4
   Total 29

4. Post and Army Work (paid)	
a. Maintenance and Supply	11
b. Post engineer	49
c. Officers' mess	3
d. Heavy duty work (salvage, lumber yard, etc.)	299
Total	362
5. Recapitulation	
a. Not available for work	24
b. Paid PW camp labor	29
c. Paid PW post and army work	362
Total	415 men

Table 5. Columbus ASF Daily Activity Report. *Courtesy of NARA, Other Inspection Reports-Perry, 1944–1945.*

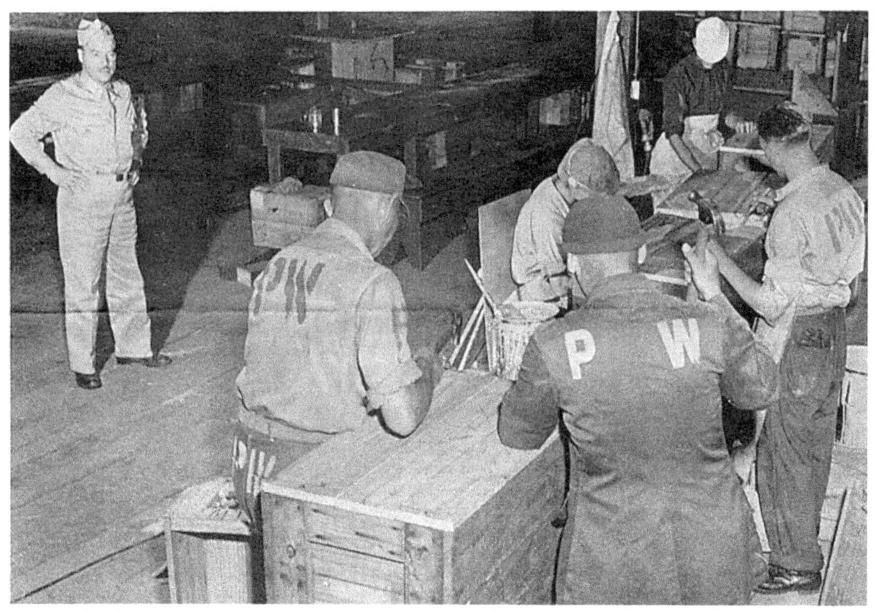

Columbus ASF Depot photo of POWs working at the depot during World War II. *Courtesy of the Whitehall Historical Society, Whitehall, Ohio.*

THOMAS A. SCOTT POW CAMP

The Thomas A. Scott POW Camp in Fort Wayne, Indiana, was established at a former training center for the army's Railroad Operating Battalions, which closed in 1944 to make room for the 640 German prisoners of war who arrived in November 1944. The German prisoners, who were part of Rommel's Afrika Korps, worked in such area industries as laundry, cleaning, stock loading and unloading, hay baling, land cleaning, warehousing, truck repair, feed handling, salvage work and steel handling, to name a few.[196]

The prisoners of war wore clothing previously worn by American servicemen, but theirs now had a large *PW* on the backs of their shirts, coats and on the seats of their pants. The clothing that they were issued included the following:[197]

1 belt	*1 pair of shoes*
2 pair of cotton socks	*4 pair of socks*
2 pair of wool trousers	*4 pair of drawers*
1 pair of gloves	*4 undershirts*
1 wool coat	*1 raincoat*
1 overcoat	*1 wool shirt*

The camp had one major incident: a German prisoner of war informed the camp commander there was going to be trouble and identified 140 potential troublemakers. The camp commander rounded up the men and had them taken to the camp theater, but this led to a rebellion that was only quelled by the guards firing over the prisoners' heads. The 140 troublemakers were sent to Camp Perry, but they had become so incorrigible that they were eventually sent to a correctional camp in Texas.[198] After the group left the camp, the labor force dropped to 500 men.

The entertainment opportunities for the German prisoners of war included soccer, a camp library, letter writing and the canteen, where the prisoners were able to purchase a bottle of 3.2 beer and two packs of cigarettes every week. Movies were shown four nights a week, and standard wave radios were available in the recreation hall. Other recreational outlets included table tennis, pool, listening to records and playing the piano. A ten-piece orchestra was formed, and paintings adorned the walls of the enlisted men's mess hall, which was operated by prisoners of war cooks and controlled by a German sergeant. An example of the daily meals is as follows:[199]

Breakfast
Coffee, fresh milk, sugar, milk with corn flakes, cake, bread

Lunch
beef broth with eggs, spaghetti, scrambled eggs, lettuce with dressing, spinach, bread, coffee milk, sugar

Supper
goulash, salt, potatoes, peas, scrambled eggs, lettuce with dressing, bread, coffee, milk, sugar

This rather robust menu of the camp gives credence to the complaints found in area newspapers alleging that the prisoners of war were eating better than Cleveland families. This sense of unfairness weaved a common thread across the United States in reaction to the rationing system, a restriction that does not seem to have been imposed on the prisoners of war at Thomas E. Scott and other area camps.

During their internment at Thomas A. Scott POW Camp, the prisoners of war were able to supply the needed help to the City of Fort Wayne's labor and community needs. The camp closed on November 16, 1945, and the remaining prisoners of war were sent back to Camp Perry.

MARION ENGINEERING DEPOT / SCIOTO ORDNANCE PLANT

At the U.S. Army's Marion Engineer Depot, the prisoners of war were housed on 24 acres within the 650-acre complex, which shipped food, supplies, military equipment and heavy renovated equipment during World War II. The depot was laid out in four avenues and six streets and had twenty-two miles of railroad track. It was the largest depot of its kind in the United States that stored and renovated heavy construction equipment for the war.[200]

The data shows that during May 1945 the depot loaded 1,544 railroad cars and unloaded 1,231 railroad cars of material and equipment. More than 1,400 civilians teamed with 295 prisoners of war to meet the labor needs of the depot.

Adjacent to the depot was the 12,000-acre Scioto Ordnance Plant, in use from 1942 to 1945. This plant had 177 magazines, 5 explosive igloos and

9 ordnance lines that manufactured bombs, fuses and boosters, including cluster and goop bombs. The Scioto Ordnance Plant produced 395 cluster bombs per day, including 38 10-pounders, each of which contained 15,000 small bombs. The cluster bomb ejected small submissions designed to kill personnel and destroy vehicles. The goop bomb was an incendiary oil- or gasoline-based bomb that was dropped in raids over Germany and Tokyo.[201] The plant employed 2,900 people who were responsible for manufacturing approximately 15.5 million fuses, 380,000 boosters, more than 2.3 million primers, 2.9 million .50-caliber rounds, 100,000 500-pound incendiary munitions and even some 10-pound incendiary cluster munitions.[202] A total of $11.2 million has been spent on the Scioto Ordnance Depot cleanup and, according to the September *Defense Environmental Programs Annual Report to Congress for FY 2014*, a cost of $1,978,000 was called for to address "newly discovered contaminants, increased physical dimensions of the cleanup, additional risk pathway such as vapor intrusion, change in future property reuse, site reopened to address additional risk and additional sampling."[203] This report is a strong indication that civilian workers, army personnel and the prisoners of war were most likely exposed to toxic working conditions at the Scioto Ordnance Plant, although one will never fully know the negative impacts it had on their health.

Daily Labor Report – April 5, 1945

PWs	Type of Work Performed
12	**PW Camp** Maintenance on compound and company area drainage.
45	**Post Engineers** Post drainage detail, maintenance, labor on Post railroad, handling, warehouse stock, blacksmith shop, paint shop and coal pile.
119	**Warehouse Operations** General police of roundhouse, stacking dunnage, assembling cable racks, upkeep of depot stock, window washing, unloading equipment, painters, salvage yard labor, processing belts, assembling cables, stacking lumber, clean-up crew and loading equipment.

PWs	Type of Work Performed
30	**Maintenance Branch** Maintenance and repair of heavy equipment, washing and lubrication of vehicles.
40	**Scioto Ordnance** Building compound at Scioto Ordnance Depot.
7	Officer's mess, K.P. work and cooking.
3	Cleaning officer's quarters and general clean-up work.
7	Post cafeteria, K.P. and general clean-up work.
4	Enlisted men's mess, K.P. and cooking.
14	PW overhead, cooks, clerks, spokesman, interpreter, supply man, canteen and director of study and latrine orderly.
14	Essential unpaid labor: K.P., barber and clean-up.
295	

Table 6. Daily Activity Labor Report, April 5, 1945. *Courtesy of NARA, RG 389, Entry 461, 1944–1945.*

In early December 1945, Camp Marion saw the arrival of 295 German prisoners of war who had served in Rommel's Afrika Korps. Camp Marion had wooden barracks and recreational areas that featured soccer and craft art, a canteen and a store where prisoners of war could use the coupons they received as work pay—equivalent to eighty cents a day—to purchase items (as discussed in chapter 6). The daily labor report of April 5, 1945, illustrates how the labor force was distributed between the engineer and the ordnance depots.[204] The prisoners of war assisted in meeting the labor needs of the two depots, and some of the prisoners eventually worked on farms in the area.

In accordance with the Geneva Convention, the War Department had declared that the prisoners of war would not be working with munitions, but it appears that at the Scioto Ordnance Plant some prisoners of war handled bomb nose pieces, tails and empty shells before being put on the assembly line. Allowing the prisoners to work side by side with civilian workers was once again due to the manpower shortage in the area.

One resident couple of Marion, Mr. and Mrs. Morehouse, used a German prisoner of war to assist them in weeding their yard and garden. The Morehouses would have the prisoner over for lunch when he worked for them and enjoyed his company. The couple remained in touch with the former German prisoner of war for several years after the war, as did a number of other Marion families with the former prisoners who helped them.[205]

In the 1960s, the River Valley Local School District built a high school and middle school on the site of the two depots, land that would later be found to be contaminated with toxic waste from chemicals buried during the production of ordnance at the depots during World War II. A high rate of leukemia and other cancers was found among former River Valley students who attended the two schools. After a bitter political battle ensued that involved a perceived cover-up, eventually the school district was awarded funds from the U.S. Army and the state's school facilities program to construct new buildings at a different site that finally opened in 2003, some seven years after the first discovery of the toxicity at the schools. The Marion Engineer Depot and Scioto Ordnance Plant were thus key distribution and bomb-making centers during World War II but became postwar tragedies wrought with political malfeasance and a lack of environmental oversight that led to local students suffering from cancer and other serious health problems.

ROSSFORD ORDNANCE DEPOT POW CAMP

The Rossford Ordnance Depot opened in 1942 and became the largest transportation depot in the United States during World War II.[206] The facility spanned more than 800 acres, was 2.5 miles long and had seventeen warehouses, three cafeterias and its own fire department. The depot was a distribution center for military vehicles, in addition to housing ammunition storage. The site had a comprehensive railroad center with a roundhouse that was key to moving military vehicles to ports across the United States for shipment to war zones overseas, as seen in the photo that shows a stockpile of jeeps for the war.[207] The Rossford Ordnance Depot, also a major center for replacement parts that were sent around the world, had its own Ordnance Parts Clerical School.

Some 659 privates and 17 officers from the 310th Quartermaster Battalion ISU were sent to the Rossford Ordnance Depot from Camp Perry in early November 1944.[208] The Italian prisoners of war were assigned to warehousing and shipping jobs, which included box-making, storing, rail maintenance and the salvaging of used materials. In the paper and lumber salvage operations,

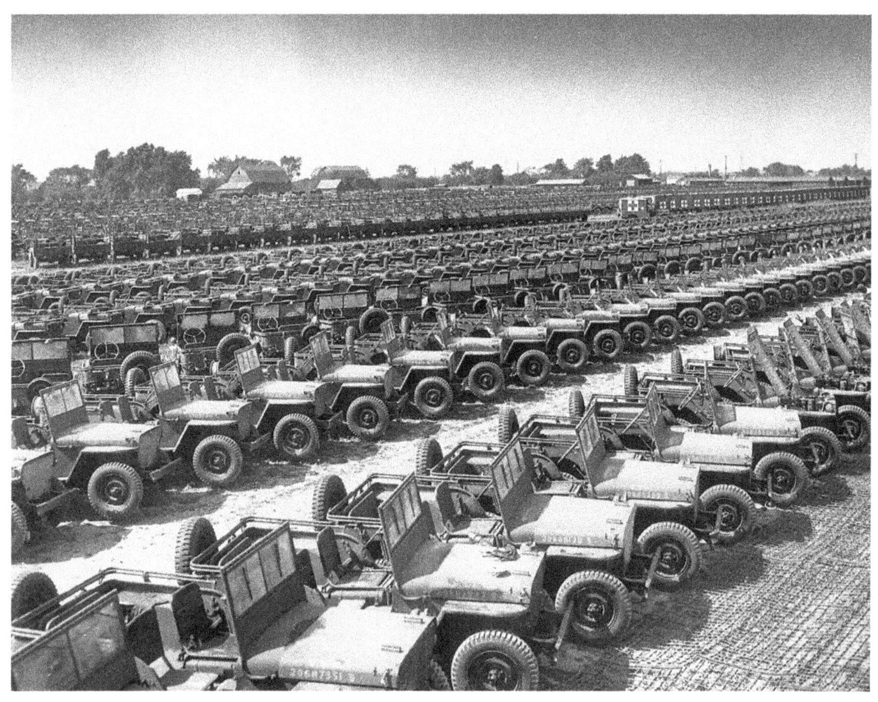

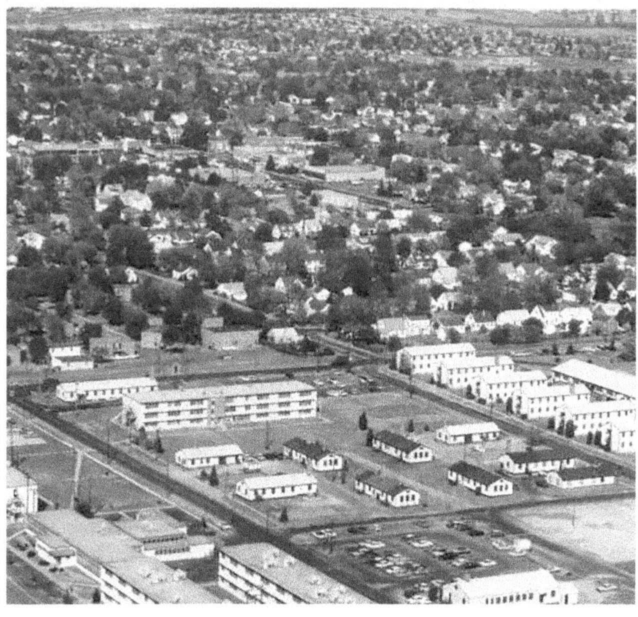

Above: Photo of the stockpile of jeeps at Rossford Ordnance Depot during World War II. *Courtesy of the Local History Department, Toledo-Lucas County Library, Toledo, Ohio.*

Left: Rossford Ordnance Depot photo of the complex during World War II. *Courtesy of the Rossford Public Library, Rossford, Ohio.*

using prisoners of war to make the shipping crates and boxes out of salvaged lumber saved the depot $3,000 a month.[209] ISU members worked alongside several thousand civilian employees at the depot.

The 310th Quartermaster Battalion was sent back to the Erie Proving Ground in mid-November 1945 for repatriation to Italy. The work of the battalion was instrumental in the successful operation of the largest vehicle distribution depot in the United States during World War II. The depot closed in 1964 and became the home of Owens Community College and Penta County Joint Vocational School.

Just as with the Marion Engineer Depot and the Scioto Ordnance Plant, the grounds of the Rossford Ordnance Depot became contaminated, as evidence by the *Defense Environmental Programs Annual Report to Congress for FY 2014*. The report stated that to clean up the Rossford Ordnance Depot, some $6,924,000 was called for because of the "added requirements due to other site-level project change because of newly discovered contaminants, increase physical dimensions of the clean-up, additions risk pathway such as vapor intrusion, change in future property reuse, site reopened to address additional risk and additional sampling."[210] Sadly, much like with the Marion Engineering Depot and Scioto Ordnance Plant, we will never truly know what the negative health impacts were on the people who worked at the site, including the prisoners of war.

OBSERVATIONS

All of the Camp Perry branch camps played a major role in meeting the manpower shortages throughout the area. In some cases, local residents befriended the prisoners and enjoyed interacting with them, but others often felt an uneasiness toward having the enemy living in their backyards and thought that the army was coddling them. This often led to hard feelings, especially among those civilians who worked side by side with the prisoners. Irrespective of one's views toward the prisoners, one had to marvel at Camp Perry's impressive administrative capabilities in its oversight of the prisoner of war labor camps, hospitals and ordnance depots.

A less admirable, and even tragic, consequence of all of the military production across Camp Perry's various branch camps was the toxic contamination that leaked into the ground of the abandoned sites. The River Valley Local District marks a sad chapter of how little the U.S. Army took into considering the negative effects that the dumping of improperly sealed chemicals and munitions would have on the property, as it failed to protect the local residents' drinking water and soil from toxic runoffs.

Based on reports from the Ohio Environmental Protection Agency, currently there are active contamination sites affecting the Erie Proving Ground, Fletcher General Hospital, Marion Engineer Depot, Scioto Ordnance Plant and Rossford Ordnance Depot. Due to its lack of foresight and understanding about toxic waste, the government has already spent millions of dollars to partially clean up the Marion, Scioto and Rossford locations with remediation that remains ongoing more than seventy years after the end of World War II. One hopes that lessons have been learned about how to more preciously preserve our local land and water, including preventive measures that work to eliminate exposure to toxic chemicals, like the kind that built up into the toxic waste dumps found at the branch camps and surrounding facilities.

11

PRISONER OF WAR UNHAPPINESS

The prisoners of war at Camp Perry and its branch camps were a challenge to manage for Lieutenant Colonel E.C. McCormick Jr. and his staff. The Italian prisoners of war became co-belligerents and, in most cases, were not a problem for camp leadership. Numerous newspaper articles referred to the Italian prisoners of war as having toothpaste smiles and carrying a happy-go-lucky disposition in the camps. The ISUs, established at Camp Perry in May 1944 as the 323rd Italian Quartermaster Battalion, were given numerous privileges, including community inspections, attendance at social gatherings with local Italian women and correspondence exceeding the quota of letters that German and non-ISU members could send back home.

The first German prisoners of war were a different story. They consisted of older men, and they were, for the most part, cooperative. However, once the Normandy prisoners of war arrived in the summer of 1944, that attitude began to change, as the more recently arrived prisoners were more wetted to the fanaticism of the Nazi regime. The hardline Nazi adherents in the camps exerted control over fellow prisoners who had drifted away from the Nazi cause through psychological intimidation and beatings with handmade weapons. The prisoners who espoused Nazi values were often called "Gestapo POWs," due to their tendency to form Nazi gangs within the camps. Similar to the system of gangs in today's prisons, the camp leadership would turn their backs on the Gestapo POWs as a means of giving them the privilege to manage their internal affairs so long as the camp could capitalize on their work productivity.

Judith M. Gansberg, in her book *Stalag U.S.A.—The Remarkable Story of German POWs in America*, writes:

> *Usually the terror was directed by "courts of honor," kangaroo courts recognized in each camp by Nazi elements. "Holy Ghost," the German Army term for severe beating, became a commonplace occurrence on the order of these courts. Many soldiers were driven to suicide to save themselves or loved ones from pain. Germans were so indoctrinated into believing the SS to be practically omnipotent that they thought almost any threat made in America could somehow be carried out in Germany. They were convinced that messages were passed in the bandages of repatriated crippled and sick prisoners, by radio, and perhaps through cooperative Americans to the SS and Gestapo in Germany.*[211]

Given that they held a more radical set of views than the Italian prisoners of war, the German prisoners of war were often the ones who escaped the camps, spurred on by their feelings of confinement, boredom, depression and homesickness. Their suicides rate, meanwhile, could be attributed to the Nazi reign of terror that pervaded the prisoner of war camps across the United States.

STRIKES

One of the first recorded strikes at Camp Perry occurred on Tuesday, July 11, 1944, when forty-eight German prisoners of war went on a sit-down strike while picking cherries on a farm near Waterville, Ohio. The prisoners wanted to earn more money for piecework and protested by eating more cherries then they were picking. The striking prisoners of war were returned to Camp Perry and placed into confinement, subject to receiving fourteen days of bread and water as permissible under an agreement between the Geneva Convention and the War Department, which oversaw the work conditions at the camp. The prisoners of war who replaced the striking prisoners were paid eighty-eight cents a day, the prevailing wage normally paid to civilians. Because civilian workers were unavailable at this time, however, the wages went instead to the prisoner of war replacement workers.[212]

Another strike occurred at Camp Perry on March 2, 1945, by 229 German prisoners of war who rebelled at what they believed was the overly harsh discipline at the camp. At the end of the strike, the prisoners were fed a bread and water diet. The day before the Camp Perry strike, 189 German prisoners of war refused to go to work at Crile General Hospital in Parma, Ohio. These striking prisoners were subsequently transported to Camp Perry and placed in solitary confinement and given the bread and water diet.[213]

A third strike occurred during the same period at Camp Perry, when 2,200 German prisoners of war went on strike, again over the perceived rigid discipline at the camp. In similar fashion, these striking prisoners were placed on a bread and water diet after their three-day strike was over, when they were forced to clean up the camp and return to their designated work at Camp Perry or their contract work outside the camp.[214] There was an additional strike at the Camp Marion Engineer Depot, this one involving 242 German prisoners of war who went on strike to protest having to work in the rain. Lieutenant Colonel E.C. McCormick Jr.'s response to the striking prisoners was to declare that they would work in rain or shine and "no work, no food," except bread and water, a move that put an end to the strike.[215]

The strikes at Camp Perry and its branch camps were consistent with the motives of the hardcore Nazi prisoners to periodically stir things up through work stoppages and their attempts to remind their American wardens who they believed was really in charge. They also desired to instill a belief in their fellow prisoners that this disruption was beneficial to the German war effort by creating a sense of confusion on enemy soil. It appears that giving the German prisoners of war authority to control their own internal workings of the camps was a means of placating the hardcore Nazis and a concession to ensure that the outside contract work was maintained, given the manpower shortage throughout the United States.

ESCAPES

Escapes at Camp Perry and its branch camps were minimal, but when they occurred and the escapees were caught, they were placed into confinement, where they received the traditional bread and water diet.

One escape happened on June 1, 1945, by a twenty-seven-year-old prisoner of war working at the Central Mills Company, a fruit-processing plant in Dunbridge, Ohio, about twenty miles south of Toledo. A June 1,

1945 *Ottawa County News* article recounted the event: "The two prisoners who escaped from a Fostoria plant last week were apprehended in downtown Columbus last Thursday. A discharged soldier recognized the GI shoes they were wearing and noticed the prisoners were crossing an intersection against a red light. They were returned to Camp Perry."[216] Fostoria is ninety-five miles outside Columbus, a considerable distance for the prisoners of war to have traveled undetected before their capture in Columbus. Another escape occurred on August 31, 1945, from Camp Perry. This time, the escapee was described as forty years old, five-feet, eleven inches tall, weighing 180 pounds, with brown hair, blue eyes and a ruddy complexion. No mention was made of when the prisoner was caught.[217]

The prisoners of war who attempted to escape all had difficulties being confined; they became bored and depressed and were spurred on by a homesickness to see their loved ones back home. In some cases, the prisoners longed to escape the Gestapo POWs at Camp Perry and its branch camps.

SUICIDES

Suicides were less common but tragically did happen at Camp Perry. An August 25, 1944 *Port Clinton Herald and Republican* article revealed that a prisoner of war had escaped from a work detail at the Defiance POW Camp and was found several hours after his disappearance drowned in the Maumee River. The prisoner of war had been sent from Camp Perry to the Defiance branch camp to work for farmers in the area.[218] Another prisoner of war who had escaped from Camp Perry on August 29, 1945, was found hanging in a tree near Willow Beach, Port Clinton, on October 5. Camp officials described him as mentally unbalanced and, until the date his body was found, the only German prisoner of war who had successfully escaped from Camp Perry.[219]

The stress of confinement and the threat of being harassed by the Gestapo POWs were too unbearable for some prisoners of war, whose fragile states deteriorated further into mental breakdowns, some so severe that they ended tragically in suicide.

OBSERVATIONS

The management routine of Lieutenant Colonel E.C. McCormick Jr. and his staff at the base and branch camps was a fine balance of maintaining discipline while providing a positive camp environment. The camp officials recognized that some of the prisoners had entered the war with reluctance and did not subscribe to Nazi ideals. Despite their best efforts to maintain a sense of order and regularity at the camp and to ensure that the prisoners were properly cared for, the stress of confinement in the camp, uncertainty over the war's outcome and pressure from hardline Nazi prisoners pushed some of the prisoners to their breaking points, leading to strikes, escape attempts and—most tragically—to some prisoners taking their own lives as the only way out.

12

CAMP PERRY NEWSPAPERS

Camp Newspaper for Camp Perry and Secondary Camp(s)
RATHER THAN NATIONALIZING HUMANS, WE'D PREFER TO HUMANIZE THE NATION
PESTALOZZI[220]
No. 2 October 6, 1945

Diktaturen betrachten unabhaengiges Denken als ihren schlimmsten Feind. Damit habin sie wehrscheinlich vollkommen recht. Tyrannei kann nur bestehen. Ssiv gehorchen. Aber solch passiver Gehorsam ist unverseinbar mit freier Intelligenz. Darum goben sich alle Tyrannen so grosse Muehe, die Intelligenz ueberhaupt zu unterdruecken oder sie nur innerhalb gewisser vorge-schriebener Grenzen zu dulden oder sie in gewisse vorbestimmte Kanaele hineinzuzwingen. Deshalb verwenden alle Diktatoren so systmmatishch das Instrument der Propaganda Fuer den Diktator sind solche unabhaengigen Intelligenzen, die Fragen stellen, hoechst gefaehrlich; den damit er sich halten kann, ist es unerlaesslich, dass die sozial anerkannten Vorurteile nicht, in Frage gestelit warden und dass die Leute ihren Witz nur dafuer verwenden, neue wirksamere Wittel zur Erreichung der Zweche aufzufinden, welch emit Diktatur vereinbar sind. Darum die Verfolgung aller mutagen Leute, das Knebeln der Presse und die systematischen Bemuehungen, mit Hilfe der Propaganda eine oeffentliche meinung zu schaeffen, welche der Tyrannei guenstig ist.

—Aldous Huxley

Translation:

Independent thinking is the greatest enemy to dictatorships; perhaps rightly so. Tyranny needs passive obedience; this, however, is incompatible with independent thinking. Tyrants use great care to categorically suppress as well as channel intelligence systematically. Thus, they regularly apply propaganda. Independent intelligence is extremely dangerous for a dictator; for, in order to survive, socially recognized prejudices must not be questioned, so that people use their humor in order to establish purposes compatible with those of a dictatorship.

—Aldous Huxley

CAMP PERRY NEWSPAPERS

The *Der Aufbau* camp newspaper was established to communicate to the German prisoners of war announcements about religious service times; the scores of soccer, chess and table tennis matches; as well as musical events and movie schedules at the camp. The newspaper also featured a puzzles corner; a humor page; a reflection section of poems and short stories; a POW corner; and editorials repudiating Nazism. The American history classes were written with the intention of acquainting the prisoners of war with the United States and American ideals and values, which in essence was a subtle Intellectual Diversion program that illustrated what it was like to live under the freedom of a democracy versus under the constraints of a dictatorship. The hope for the re-education program was that it would repatriate the prisoners of war so that, when they went home, they would be instilled with democratic concepts they had learned in class and work to rebuild Germany's system of government.

Translations of the October 6, December 8 and December 15, 1945 editions of *Der Aufbau* provide examples of the German sense of humor, poems, short stories, updates on camp activities and editorials repudiating Nazism that were often found in the newspaper. The change in feeling by the Camp Perry German prisoners of war toward the war is evident in a May 11, 1945 *Ottawa County News* article, "German Prisoners at Camp Perry Were Not Surprised at Surrender—Now They Talk Freely, Camp Commander Says."[221] Lieutenant Colonel McCormick Jr. is quoted as saying: "The first effect of the last week preceding V-E Day was that

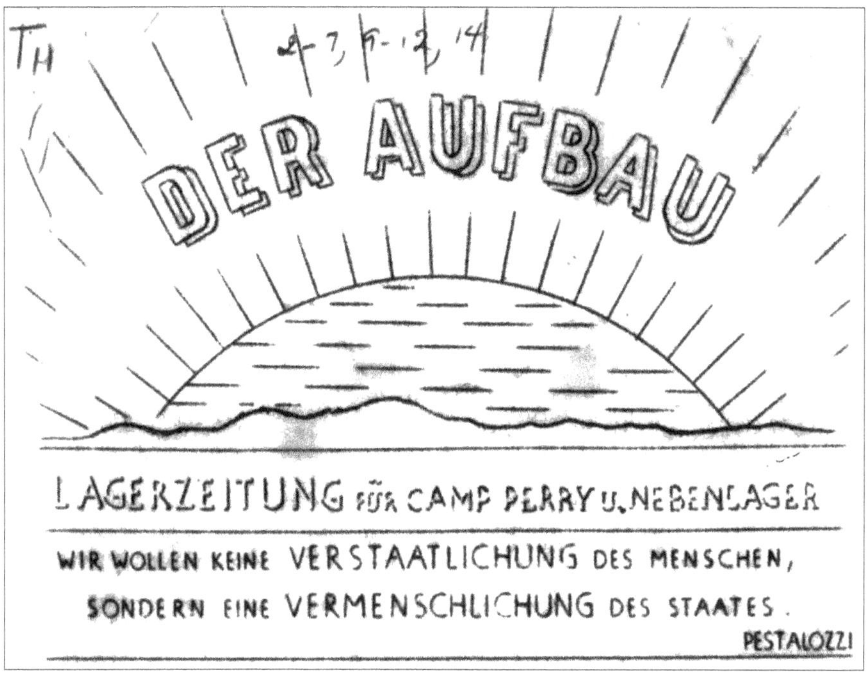

Der Aufbau newspaper at Camp Perry, October 6, 1945. *Courtesy of author's collection.*

the PW's started to talk more freely. The men, who for many years were secret opponents of the Hitler regime spoke-up first. These men were happy and jubilant on V-E Day, and as one of them stated, 'Our hopes have come true.'"

One interesting editorial entitled "Hinderberg Last Will and Testament," by a Camp Perry prisoner of war, lays out in detail Hitler's rise to power and the destruction of an enlightened German culture that saw the disappearance of its constitution and rule of law.

The following sections have been translated from the Camp Perry *Der Aufbau* newspapers distributed at the base camp and supporting branch camps. The translated sections of the newspapers provide a picture of camp life and the feelings of the prisoners of war after Germany surrendered on May 7, 1945.

GERMAN POW COMIC RELIEF

Der Aufbau
December 15, 1945:

General Keitel *has a conversation with the Director Furtwaengler during the intermission of one of the Berlin Philharmonics concerts. After a while Furtwaengler asked Keitel, whom he knew very well, why the sudden set-back after the victorious advances in Russia. Keitel answered, "If Hitler knew how to play the harmonica, you not be director any longer."*[222]

Dr. Joseph Goebbels, *that famous defender of truth and honor, announced on radio in October 1941: "The Russian army has been destroyed." Several months later there circulated a cartoon in Germany, showing the famous Dr. Goebbels, while standing in a foxhole and holding a placard reading: "Russians, you have ceased to exist." Directly behind him it showed a typical Junkerofficer whispering to a General, who appeared to be starving: "These stupid Russians seem not to understand one word of German."*[223]

Water and Wine:[224] *On a hot summer day, Goethe Johann Wolfgang von Goethe, 1759–1832, greatest author and poet of German language, asked for a bottle of wine and a bottle of water in a local pub, to quench his thirst. From the next table, a group of merry students finally sent one of their group to ask politely, why he would dilute that fine wine with ordinary water.*

I shall give the gentlemen a written report. He very hastily scribbled a few words on a piece of paper and soon did send the note to the next table. With great humiliation they read:

Water alone makes one mute
as proven by fish in water.
Wine pure makes one stupid
as proven by the gentlemen at the next table
But, since I don't want to be either,
I mix water with wine.

The Thing with Kieselack by Willem Jasport:[225] *In the last century, there lived a man in Vienna by the name of Kieselack. He had the most obsessive-compulsive habit to write his name on anything and everything. Into tree barks on the Prater-Haupt-Allee, at restaurants in Grinzing, (wine entertainment center) on Kallenberg (park), street cars, theaters, even at the Portal of Hofburg. That was too much. Complaints reached the police, City Administrators, Ministry of the Interior. The Marshall of the Imperial Court finally had to report this to the Emperor himself. He himself chided Kieselack duly and threatened prison time if this did not stop. With this, he was dismissed. However, the Emperor was astonished when he noticed "Kieselack" inscribed in the corner of his own heavy oak desk. Years later, after Kieselack's death and during an unusual drought, the level of the Danube River fell lower than many inhabitants could remember. And at that time, huge, flat stones emerged in the river bed with huge, engraved letters, legible from afar.*

Der Aufbau
October 6, 1945:

Kieselack
Repudiation of Nazism
How We Were Deceived[226]

The German political party declared: "We are the State." After capitulation, the "Little man" asked: "How could all this happen? Why didn't I realize all this deception before?" NSDAP (Nazi Party) had promised everyone, what he or she had wanted to hear. This new State will meet the needs of the people! Organizations were created for every person and every level of the population, disguised as "Service" for the State. Uniforms were created for every organization, thus people were duped into "feeling important, feeling needed" in this new State. Neighbors were able to observe who does service? This is how "Nationalization of Humans" was accomplished.

With great astonishment did we see here in the U.S. that everyday things, which had been promised us, were the norm here; e.g., a general had to answer in Washington his behavior to a common soldier at the front. Citizens lived much freer here. In the U.S. government measures were discussed as well as criticized simultaneously. In Reichstag, no discussion. "Rise meant: Measure, law, etc. passed, was accepted. No Objection."

POWs are now asking, "Why were war criminals allowed to die, and we are forced to live on.?

Let's Not Forget:[227] *According to the statement by officials in 1933, "conditions after 1918 (loss of WW I) were chaotic." Really??? Reconstruction of Germany after 1918 would only be possible with the help of countries. However, these countries needed a guarantee that any assistance be used for people and business. Not for re-establishing a military state.*

The Weimer Republic rebuilt Germany to be recognized again. It established lasting, social regulations: eight-hour work days, labor laws, health and old-age protections etc. Yet, for such democratic achievements some groups had "national" goals: defense organizations to prove to the world that Germany is not beaten militarily. Such organizations facilitated the rise of Hitler and his goals—military rule in Germany and rule over other people.

When time comes to re-organize a new Germany, we need to remember who had gotten Germany in the most horrible of all wars! Again, help from other countries to rebuild for the German people, not military goal!
—Rudolf Jerrentrup, Camp Perry

Der Aufbau
December 15, 1945:

Der Aufbau
Newspaper for Camp Perry and Outlying Camps[228]

The high hope, that the rebuilding of Germany happens satisfactorily (succeeds successfully) and that the German people will be able to play an appropriate, economical, as well as cultural role in other peoples' lives is not in the realm of party politics.

This hope is based on the integrity of those powers, as opposed to the changing, political prevailing trend—which I call the "Eternal Germany," the Germany of great poets and thinkers, the Germany, which gave the concept of world events to peoples' lives and applied itself for human duties (responsibilities).

If these powers awaken out of the current disease and sorrows to elementary energy, then one does not have to fear that a new German life will come forth out of these difficult (unfortunate) conditions of the current rebuilding that will be meaningful as well as inspiring for other people.
—Max Fischer

POW Boulevard:[229] *I have it from a reliable source, my friend's friend, he is working outside (out of the camp) for American, he heard that all POWs will go to France, they leave New York and go to Le Havre. And from there to the Bretagne. And after one year, home, that is, only who behaves well. That is not a rumor, I know that. My friend's friend, he works outside.*

And the Sargent detailed me to work. What a nuisance! And the other one was lying on his bed! Well, things may go differently sometime.

And then it's eleven o'clock and all the chimneys begin to smoke. And in expectation of lunch, all POW problems are forgotten until tomorrow morning during the next POW walk, on POW Boulevard at a quarter to nine.

Der Aufbau
December 8, 1945:

Summary of Hitler's Rise to Power
Hindenburg's Last Will and Testament:[230]

Let's remember: Hindenburg died on August 2, 1934, the last, constitutionally elected Reichspresident. The Constitution of the Weimar Republic had prescribed the President of the Reich's Justice Department to take over the business of Reichspresident until a successor is elected. The Reich's Cabinet was to call for new election. Instead, Hitler, who had been Reich Chancellor until then, immediately took the position of Reichspresident himself and called himself now "Fuehrer and Chancellor of the German Reich and People."

To give the union of these two offices a legitimate appearance, Hitler wanted the German People to show its agreement of disagreement by an election on August 19. Shortly before this election, on August 15, an official document "Political Testament" from Hindenburg was made public that clearly declared the German People may acknowledge Hitler unconditionally as its Fuehrer and give him its full trust. As expected, the absolute majority voted for Hitler. The "Yes-Sayer" lay in the 80–90% or higher. This percentage became characteristic in German elections. The path for "total" seizure of power by National Socialism had been laid.

Only a few weeks before, end of June or beginning of July 1934, Hitler's position had not been cemented yet. The Roehm-Revolt unquestionably was an inner disintegration-crisis of the party. Hitler managed to put it down only with enormous power. He used that opportunity to get rid of other men also, who somehow were standing in his way. However, possibly the most important outcome of the Roehm-Revolt (assassinated leader Ernst Rohm) was the downfall of the SA (storm troopers), who until then, had been the "Political Soldiers." It never regained its power. In its place now moved, until little noticed, the SS (political soldiers of the Nazi party). This was the purest embodiment of national-socialistic wishes.

Many of the German People had been deeply shaken by the Rehm-Putsch and the gruesome bloodbath of its derailing. Who would have thought at that time that this was only a prelude? Reasons, scope, and goal of this conspiracy remain a puzzle. While the economic situation was somewhat depressed due to Hitler's foreign trade policy, and the secure foundation of the Constitution had been removed, the people now could see, with shudders, what upheavals such "Palace Revolts" by the current power brokers could cause.

The actual of Hitler's election was by no one's account as favorably as was officially reported. For the first time, election fraud had been employed locally, upon orders from above, in order to match the high percentage points reported in Hitler's favor.

Hitler's Foreign Policy was equally unfavorable. The Putsch (overthrow) of the National Socialist in Austria, initiated by him, ended with the murder of Federal Chancellor Dollfuss, but revolt was a total failure. The first meeting between Hitler and Mussolini in Venice, shortly before the Roehm Revolt, was also a total failure. That is the reason why Hitler did not feel quite secure as head of state, even while he had amassed all the power in his hands.

The Saar-Question (plebiscite returned to Germany) was another topic for Foreign Policy decisions; the first major problem since the seizure of power that could turn out to be the test for European peace. It became absolutely necessary for Hitler to convince many circles and other people in the German government that he would be the only person who could lead the German people. He needed to secure his position. So, Hindenburg's death became a favorable factor in Hitler's "career." Officially it was published and discussed in newspapers and radio to no end. German masses were literally pummeled with this providence. All schools had to dedicate one full hour to this topic and read that "document" verbatim.

"Hindenburg's political testament?" Many a person had asked half doubtingly. Most of them were never fully convinced that everything had

gone the right way. What is a political testament? This was an often-asked question at that time and today, in Nuremberg Trials, it is asked again. We are familiar with Testaments of this kind from statesmen and rulers in Europe who discuss only political and governmental questions of the future of their states and who want to give advice to their successors, as opposed to testaments of their private affairs.

Emperor Karl V, the French Minister Richelieu, Frederick the Great left important thoughts in this form. Usually men and women did this to secure or intend to secure the power base of the state. We are also aware of counterfeit testaments; they were used for certain political purposes. The most familiar one is the testament of Peter the Great. Napoleon used this to expose Russian politics around 1810 as well as to prepare his attack on Russia diplomatically.

It was reserved for Adolf Hitler to go back again to this reprehensible method of forging. One of the first, great (important, meaningful) revelations at the Nuremberg Trials cleared the question of Hindenburg's testament by Franz von Papen's, vice chancellor, testimony once and forever.

We now know that by having constitutionally carried on his office and by his character, by his extensive reputation within Germany and in foreign countries, he abused Hindenburg's name and personality for the reason to reach his goal by his own desire for power. Hitler proclaimed in Hindenburg's name exactly what he himself had desired, thus deceiving the German people and the entire world. He said of everything the opposite of what Hindenburg had in his own, real testament, which had never been published. Franz von Papen had reconstructed Hindenburg's testament verbatim, from which we now see that Hindenburg had serious doubts about Hitler's further development and he probably thought he would be able to warn him, even after his own death.

Hitler, being a ruthless usurper, disregarded everything. He united the legislature and executive powers in his hands through an audacious deception; later he added the highest, the judicial power as well. With that act, the development which Germany had taken, along with other cultural states within the past 200 years to be a rule of law and a constitutional state, was destroyed. Everything still happened within the German borders. Hitler instituted compulsory military service in March 1935. Exactly one year later he broke with the Lucarno Pact of October 1925, saying that Germany would never go to war and "began to make European History." The end of that "Meteoric Career" ended May 1945 with the German capitulation.
—Friedrich Facius, Camp Perry

OBSERVATIONS

The December 15, 1945 edition of *Der Aufbau* was published two months before the last German prisoners of war left Camp Perry on February 15, 1946. The translated *Der Aufbau* newspapers were published by German prisoners of war, showing that they were unafraid of any repercussions from fellow prisoners in the repudiation of Nazism and in the descriptions of how the German people had lost their freedoms that once existed. Now was the time to restore their cultural heritage and rebuild the infrastructure of Germany so that it could once again become an economic and social leader among the free societies in the twentieth century and beyond.

13

CAMP PERRY AREA RESIDENTS' REMEMBRANCES

Residents in the Port Clinton area had varied remembrances of the prisoners of war as it pertains to how they were transported to and from work, working on the farm, the Erie Proving Ground, prisoner of war attitudes and even a chance encounter after the war. The following remembrances were compiled by the Ottawa County Historical Museum from responses by area residents who had a connection to the prisoners of war at Camp Perry and the Erie Proving Ground.

TRANSPORTATION TO AND FROM WORK

Dan Rhodes lived on his family farm in Catawba Island, Ohio, during World War II. He remembers when his father went to Camp Perry and picked up at least five prisoners of war in a red flatbed 34 truck, but in most cases, they preferred that the farmers take ten prisoners. Each group of prisoners had one guard. The prisoners of war received a five-minute break each hour, and they took a forty-minute break at noon. At the end of the day, his father would drive them back to Camp Perry.

Marvin Gackstetter remembers the prisoners of war being brought to the tomato fields with a driver and a guard, and he never witnessed any problems.

Bob and Dorothy Oherhaus were associated with the Peninsula Transportation Service, where they transported Italian and German prisoners of war to and from Camp Perry for work. Although they drove long hours, they were thankful for the work. The couple remembers buses running out of Oak Harbor, where drivers would keep the buses on their farms so they were ready to transport the prisoners to the various worksites.

FARM WORK

Lloyd Dayton lived on a farm in Danbury, Ohio, and assisted his dad with the farm work. After high school, Lloyd joined the navy, and the only help available at the time was from the prisoners of war at Camp Perry. Five prisoners of war—under the watchful eye of a guard—picked peaches on his father's farm for one week, the allotted timeframe given to his father by the War Department and Camp Perry.

Marvin Gackstetter recalls that at noon the prisoners of war from Camp Perry would sit at one end of the field and eat their packed lunches and tomatoes from the fields. They had a jar of water and were allowed to drink when they had accomplished a certain amount of work. Marvin said, "there were no bathroom facilities, so they just roughed it the best they could."

Kandace York remembers the German prisoners of war from Camp Perry on their farm during World War II. She recalls one story in particular about her mother, Lily Ann: "Ma made extra food for them and talked to them to try to make them feel at home. They used to sing while they worked on our farm. One of the songs was 'Lili Marleen.'"

ERIE PROVING GROUND

Dorothy Ostling worked at the Erie Proving Ground and says that when the first prisoners of war arrived, they realized that they were safe and sound while our guys were still overseas being shot at, which was hard to accept. The Italian prisoners of war swept the grounds and picked up papers, etc. They worked in the PX inside Gate I, which was like a big cafeteria and also had gift shops. The cafeteria was inside Gate II, where the Italians served as waiters.

ATTITUDES

Tom Lane remembers the prisoners of war as being happy, because in his mind he thought they did not want to go back and fight but just wanted to wait it out until the end of the war. He said that we assumed they were friendly, and he observed that they were more than willing to work.

Dan Rhodes assumed that the German prisoners of war were monstrous, were very difficult and looked like everyone else except that they spoke a different language and did not joke or smile a lot. Dan goes on to say that the German prisoners of war were good workers but always looked very gloomy, compared to the Italians, who laughed a lot, were more jovial and were accepted by the people in town. The Italian prisoners of war had many descendants in the area, and he enjoyed eating with them, where they would wear white hats, white t-shirts, white aprons, hold their hands behind their backs and always be laughing.

Dorothy Ostling, who worked at the Erie Proving Ground, says that the Italian prisoners of war were very friendly and some of them spoke good English, which left a good impression on her.

Bob Schraidt says that you could tell the Germans from the Italians because the Italians were laid-back and so friendly, while the Germans were stoic and stern and did not talk much, although they worked hard.

CHANCE ENCOUNTER

Janet Stephenson recalls that around 1970 she went to East Germany and had a tour guide in East Berlin who was assigned by the East German government. She said that she was from Port Clinton, Ohio, and discovered that her tour guide had been a prisoner of war at Camp Perry. The tour guide was delighted to reminisce about his time at Camp Perry, and she felt that he must have remembered the pleasant things from his time at the camp.

OBSERVATIONS

Transporting the prisoners of war to and from work provided jobs for area residents who were unemployed, while the prisoners of war filled the void of a labor shortage during the peak harvest season on area farms. The differences in attitudes between the German and Italian prisoners of war, as remembered by the area residents, matches what was reported in local newspapers and reinforces the sense of fear and intimidation that reportedly ran through the camps and was propagated by some of the hardline Nazis. The Italian prisoners of war, because they became co-belligerents and were a happy-go-lucky lot who received extended privileges at the Erie Proving Ground—including side trips to Port Clinton, Sandusky and Toledo—were able to host social gatherings at the proving ground. The chance encounter is illustrative of how some prisoners of war adjusted to their confinement and, when repatriated, were thankful for how humanely they were treated.

14
CAMP PERRY AND THE GENEVA CONVENTION (1929)

In a review of inspection reports from the National Archives and Records Administration and newspaper articles from towns in the vicinity of Camp Perry, it is evident that the camp commander, Lieutenant Colonel E.C. McCormick Jr., followed the articles of the Geneva Convention in overseeing the operation of the camp as it pertained to the treatment of the prisoners of war. Some of the procedures implemented by the lieutenant colonel to abide by the Geneva Convention included the following: prohibiting officers from working unless they requested to work; allowing noncommissioned officers to engage in only supervisory work; permitting only those physically able to do the work; and ensuring that the prisoners of war received the mandated ten cents a day allowance and eighty cents a day for labor, which in most cases was redeemed by the prisoners in the form of coupons at the camp canteen.

The following section outlines the main articles of the Geneva Convention and analyzes the degree to which the Camp Perry operation adhered to the articles, based on various points of research.

Article 10—Lodging: The barracks met the articles of the Geneva Convention for adequate housing by providing hutments that adequately housed five prisoners of war each and were sufficiently winterized with double walls and double windows, as well as containing wood-burning stoves properly ventilated through the ceiling.

Article 11—Food: The prisoners of war were required to receive food equivalent in quantity and quality to that of the depot troops, which raised some objection among Port Clinton residents because, in some cases, the prisoners of war were receiving brand-name foods that even the residents were not receiving. Numerous newspaper articles at the time indicated that this kind of action by Camp Perry was another example of coddling the prisoners of war.

Article 12—Clothing: Early inspection reports indicate that the enlisted men's clothing was being marked but that there was a shortage of work gloves, but this was eventually corrected.

Article 13—Hygiene: The inspection reports state that the sanitary conditions of Camp Perry were above reproach.

Article 14—Medical Care: According to the inspection reports, the stockade had two dispensaries equipped to provide medical services to patients who did not require hospitalization and a post hospital just outside the stockade to meet the medical needs of more serious patients. One inspection report indicates that the dental needs of the prisoners of war were met by the post hospital; however, there were complaints from the German prisoners of war of insufficient dental work related to the supply of dentures because preference was given to the American troops destined for overseas duty. Optical services, meanwhile, were provided by the post hospital.

Article 15—Medical Inspections: The monthly inspection reports reveal that Camp Perry met and exceeded the medical requirements for the prisoners of war by having two dispensaries and a post hospital that were fully staffed to meet the medical needs of the prisoners of war.

Article 16—Religion: A designated area was set aside at the camp for hosting religious activities, both initially, when the camp housed the Italian prisoners of war, and later, when the German prisoners of war replaced the Italians. A U.S. chaplain priest and local padre provided Mass for the Italian prisoners of war at the camp, and when the German prisoners replaced the Italian prisoners, a Catholic priest was assigned who spoke German. However, the German prisoners of war nonetheless protested that they did not have any German chaplains.

Article 17—Intellectual and Sporting Pursuits: In the early stages of the camp, some of the Italians were taught English. In February 1945, Dean Carter of the University of Toledo pledged full cooperation in implementing an educational program and furnishing the camp with textbooks for the classes to be offered. The German prisoners of war at Camp Perry and at many of the branch camps were given the option of taking English or American history, courses that were viewed by some as acting more akin to an indoctrination program that may have violated the intent of Article 17

(Intellectual Pursuits), not only at Camp Perry but also at other prisoner of war camps across the United States. The inspection reports state that Camp Perry had ample room and facilities for indoor and outdoor recreation activities and had all the athletic equipment needed to satisfy the needs of the prisoners of war.

Article 18—Responsible Officer: Lieutenant Colonel E.C. McCormick Jr. was the commanding officer of the camp, and an American officer was assigned to each of the prisoner of war companies.

Article 19—Badges and Decorations: Various photographs of the prisoners of war at Camp Perry demonstrate that the camp adhered to Article 19.

Article 20—Announcements: One of the inspection reports suggested that more locations ought to be designated within the camp for announcement purposes, a proposal that was acted upon after the issuance of the report.

Article 21—Officers and Enlisted Men: The inspection reports state that there was segregation between the officers and enlisted men, and when any subversive activities arose by the camp prisoners, those prisoners were transferred to other camps, where they were held in strict confinement.

Article 27—Labor Utilized According to Rank and Aptitude: Noncommissioned officers performed only supervisory work, although some officers requested to do work requiring remuneration for services rendered, which had been approved by Lieutenant Colonel McCormick.

Article 28—Working for Private Individuals: The contract with Harry Engleback of Port Clinton, Ohio, is an example of Camp Perry following the articles of the Geneva Convention as it pertained to working with private individuals and industries.

Article 29—Physically Fit for Work: Lieutenant Colonel MCormick Jr., in his memorandums to staff, emphasized that the prisoners of war must be physically fit for work.

Article 30—Duration of Work: Also, in his memorandums, the lieutenant colonel continually emphasized that, unless it was an emergency situation, the prisoners of war were prohibited from working ten-hour days and each week were entitled to a rest period lasting twenty-four consecutive hours, preferably on Sundays.

Article 31—Arms and Munitions Work: The prisoners of war were not allowed to work directly with munitions, but ISU members working at the Erie Proving Ground could salvage artillery equipment.

Article 33—Labor Detachments: The inspection reports consistently attest that Camp Perry met Class I labor requirements for prisoners in the stockade and Class II labor requirements for outside contract work.

Article 34—Non-Payment and Payment of Wages: Lieutenant Colonel E.C. McCormick Jr., through memorandums to staff, made it clear that Class I labor internees who were assigned to camp operations were not to be paid, while those internees who were assigned to outside contract work (Class II labor) were to be paid wages outlined by the War Department.

Article 36—Sending Letters and Postcards: Limitations on the length and quantity of letters and postcards imposed on the prisoners met the intent of Article 36. The camp also maintained a censoring system to ensure that the prisoners of war did not send or receive subversive material. Prisoners of war who were ISU members were given the privilege of exceeding the quota of what non-ISU members and German prisoners of war could send back home.

Article 37—Receiving of Foodstuffs: Camp Perry followed the Geneva Convention requirements by instituting a policy that stated the prisoners of war could receive foodstuffs and articles intended for consumption and clothing so long as the parcel did not exceed four pounds.

OBSERVATIONS

Various points of research indicate that Lieutenant Colonel E.C. McCormick Jr. and his staff operated an orderly camp that imposed a firm but fair discipline. Officials clearly outlined what the camp's expectations were for the prisoners. The inspection reports and local newspaper articles substantiate the claim that Camp Perry was adhering to the articles of the Geneva Convention in its treatment of the prisoners of war, despite the claims made by an increasingly hostile and confrontational group of some German camp prisoners who believed the camp was failing to do so. Perhaps the one program made by camp officials that deserves further scrutiny is the re-education program and determining whether its attempt to subversively undercut the hardline Nazi viewpoints that ran rampant in the camp and replace them with American ideals and values violated Article 17 (Intellectual Pursuits).

15

CONTAMINATION ON THE HOME FRONT

A story that was seemingly buried beneath the surface of the research into Camp Perry and its surrounding prisoner of war branch camps soon began to be revealed. The land on which the various facilities was located—namely, the Erie Proving Ground, Fletcher General Hospital, Marion Engineering Depot, Rossford Ordnance Depot and Scioto Ordnance Plant—has been shown to be significantly contaminated with high levels of toxic waste. In response, major cleanup projects have been launched, funded by Formerly Used Defense Site (FUDs) programs that identify sites and categorize the types of hazards according to the following categories:[231]

BD/DR = Building Demolition and Debris Removal
CON/HTRW = Containerized Hazardous, Toxic and/or Radioactive Waste
HTRW = Hazardous, Toxic and/or Radioactive Waste
MMRP = Military Munitions Response Program
MMRP/CWM = Military Munitions Response Program/Chemical Warfare Materials
PRP/HTRW = Potentially Responsible Party Actions/Hazardous, Toxic and/or Radioactive Waste
PRP/MMRP = Potentially Responsible Party Actions/Military Munitions Response Program

Property	City	County	Site	Category
Erie Army Depot	Port Clinton	Ottawa	00	CON/ HTRW
Erie Army Depot	Port Clinton	Ottawa	03	HTRW
Erie Army Depot	Port Clinton	Ottawa	05	PRP/ HTRW
Erie Army Depot	Port Clinton	Ottawa	06	MMRP
Erie Army Depot	Port Clinton	Ottawa	12	CON/ HTRW
Erie Army Depot	Port Clinton	Ottawa	13	HTRW
Erie Army Depot	Port Clinton	Ottawa	14	PRP/ HTRW
Fletcher General Hospital	Cambridge	Guernsey	02	CON/ HTRW
Marion Eng. Depot	Marion	Marion	02	CON/ HTRW
Marion Eng. Depot	Marion	Marion	03	HTRW
Rossford AD	Rossford	Wood	00	MMRP
Rossford AD	Rossford	Wood	01	HTRW
Rossford AD	Rossford	Wood	02	HTRW
Rossford AD	Rossford	Wood	03	CON/ HTRW
Scioto Ordnance Plant	Marion	Marion	02	CON/ HTRW
Scioto Ordnance Plant	Marion	Marion	03	HTRW
Scioto Ordnance Plant	Marion	Marion	06	MMRP

Table 7. Formerly used defense sites in Ohio affiliated with Camp Perry. *Courtesy of the U.S. Army Corps of Engineers, FUDS Inventory, 2015.*

The Erie Proving Ground (also known as the Erie Army Depot) has removed munitions along its eight-mile shoreline and its subsurface and undertook environmental remediation at a cost of $3,873,000 as of July 31,

2001, while an additional $624,000 is needed for future work.[232] In the end, approximately $8.2 million was spent on the cleanup and munitions removal at the Erie Army Depot (Erie Proving Ground).[233]

As discussed in chapter 3, there have been more than eight thousand ordnances removed from the Lake Erie shoreline, only a fraction of all the ordnance fired into Lake Erie. An Ohio EPA report warns of future problems of a landfill on the site of the old Erie Proving Ground:

> *Contaminants known and suspected in Lake Erie and the surrounding soil are directly related to chemicals used in the production and firing of ordnance. Contamination from the landfill includes known and suspected components. Currently the landfill has a soil cover, but no liner of leachate collection system. The landfill is surrounded on two sides by drainage ditches which run into Lake Erie, thus there is potential for contamination of ground water, surface water and adjoining properties.*[234]

Conversations with the Ohio EPA reveal that the agency is concerned about the landfill and will continue to monitor it.

The River Valley Local School District built its high school and middle school on seventy-eight acres on the site of the old Marion Engineering Depot in the early 1960s, but it was not until the 1990s that residents of the district began to link the high rates of leukemia, Non-Hodgkin Lymphoma and other forms of cancer that were found to be prevalent among the graduates to the activities of the former depot.[235] The schools were built on the same area that was formerly used for heavy equipment and training, materials storage, burial of construction debris and depot waste and the burning of waste material and fuels. A radium-painted, dime-sized aluminum disc was found just below the soil on the front lawn of the high school, a marker the army used to indicate the position of bridges and vehicles while troops were practicing nighttime operations. Other tests at the school site indicate the presence of volatile organic compounds in both the soil and perched groundwater on school property. Vats of chemical residues were buried in trenches covered with soil, over which the school built its athletic fields, unaware of the toxic danger, which led to citizen outrage and concern for the health of the students.[236]

Another grave concern is the discovery of arsenic in the drainage ditches along both sides of a former railroad spur where prisoners of war were dropped off during World War II upon their arrival at the Marion Engineer Depot camp. Apparently, it was here the prisoners of war were sprayed with an arsenic-laden delousing agent upon exiting from railroad cars known to be treated with an arsenic-bearing fumigant still present at elevated levels fifty years later. Most alarming are the eleven chemicals found above reporting limits and six TAL metals (exhibit metallic properties) that were detected above site-specific background levels[237] at the Marion Engineering Depot.

A *Columbus Dispatch* article of October 17, 1997, was titled, "Leukemia News Stuns Marion—Death Rates Up 122% in 30 Years, State Study Finds." The accompanying chart, Tracking a Killer, was done by the state health department, comparing the number of leukemia deaths in three 10-year periods in the city of Marion's population of 34,075 and Marion County's population of 94,274, where 151 deaths occurred from leukemia from 1966 to 1995. The Marion County population number does not include the population of Marion City. It was noted in the article that the death rate from leukemia in Ohio for the same period was only 8 percent.[238]

This alarming comparison led to concern across the region and state, especially among the families of the students who had graduated and those attending the River Valley Local School District. Proactive measures were undertaken by the Concerned River Valley Families group, which periodically ran ads stating that more than seventy cancers had been reported to the

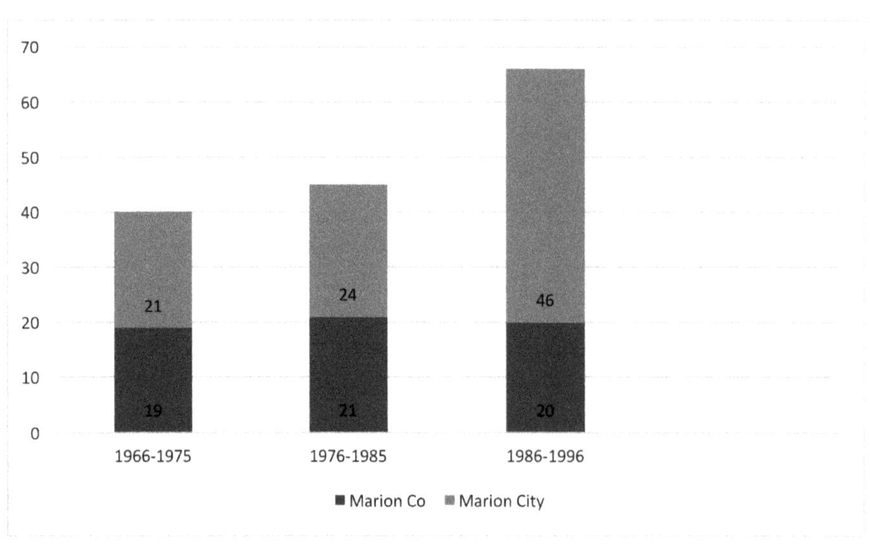

Chart 11. Tracking a Killer. *Courtesy of the Department of Army,* Columbus Dispatch, *October 17, 1997.*

group. The group's members feared that there may be some unreported cases. The title of their ads was "River Valley Graduates and Families, We Need Your Help."[239]

The removal of the chemicals and hazardous waste at the school district site has cost $5,773,000 as of a July 31, 2001 report,[240] and in the end, approximately $35.7 million was spent on the cleanup of the former Marion Engineer Depot grounds.[241] The schools were finally closed and rebuilt in different locations in 2003 at a cost of $52,929,197, including a $7,985,100 match from the Ohio School Facilities Commission, $29,964,000 from the passage of a local bond issue and a $15,000,000 contribution from the U.S. Army Corps of Engineers. Health officials were not able to determine whether or not the contaminated soil contributed to the various forms of cancer that afflicted the graduates. Today, the vacated buildings are being used as private warehousing facilities with the site being tested every five years.

The *Columbus Dispatch* reporter Dan Narciso wrote an article on May 31, 2017, entitled "Questions Linger decades after River Valley Cleanup," in which he reported, "Today many of those who fought for more studies, accountability and justice feel that their happy high school memories have been dampened by what was buried under their playing fields." In the article, a former student indicated that "years of cross country, track and cheerleading put her in almost daily contact with the often-soggy school grounds," and another former student believes that public pressure stopped further investigations as it pertained to possible links of the contaminated school site to the high rate of cancer among former students.[242] It is clear that the River Valley Local School District tragedy is an unfortunate legacy that will be with the community forever.

The Scioto Ordnance Plant, located adjacent to the Marion Engineering Depot, also left behind toxic debris, with portions of the depot fenced off from public access. Lagoons and dumps have been discovered laden with concrete, bricks and burned materials on top of M-74 bomblets and incendiary petroleum-based fuels, including burned napalm. Other environmental remediation efforts have included removing close to three thousand M-74 bomblets, live M-142 fuses and 3,995 pounds of munitions debris.[243] A July 31, 2001 GAO report shows that $3,605,000 has been spent on the cleanup, and an additional $12,557,000 is projected for future remediation.[244] The Department of Defense *Environmental Restoration Program FY 2015 Report* indicated that $11,331,000 has been spent on cleanup with an additional $255,000 for continued cleanup.[245]

The *Fiscal Year 2015 Defense Environmental Status of Installation Program Report* indicated that $974,000 had been spent on the Rossford Ordnance Depot cleanup and an additional $23,000 needed for continued cleanup.[246] There are still buildings from the Rossford Ordnance Depot on the site; the question is whether or not they are being used by the Penta County Joint Vocational School and Owen Community College. If so, this calls into question the environmental safety of the Penta County Joint Vocational School and Owens Community College students, raising fears that the schools may be sitting on toxic waste dumps/burn pits, and, if so, what the health impacts are on current and former students.

OBSERVATIONS

It is evident that the U.S. Army's operating procedures during World War II were focused on winning the war overseas and did not take into adequate consideration the negative effects that the burning and burial of toxic chemicals would have on the environment. Tragically, this lack of foresight has led to numerous long-term health impacts on people who worked at the depots during World War II and their future generations, including students of the River Valley School District and now possibly the Penta County Joint Vocational School and Owens Community College. One wonders what the deleterious health effects were for the prisoners of war, the civilians and the army personnel who worked at these locations; in particular, those prisoners who were doused with arsenic solutions and workers who inhaled chemical solutions. The U.S. war effort may have inadvertently contributed to the health problems and even deaths of those closest to home due to a lack of understanding of the danger and long-term impact that the unregulated dumping of toxic chemicals had at these facilities so vital to the war production effort.

16

CAMP PERRY IN REVIEW

The Ohio National Guard's Camp Perry Joint Training Site remains a vibrant facility dedicated to the training of troops and law enforcement personnel, in addition to serving as a recreation destination for enjoyment by the public. Planning and construction of the camp began in 1905; by September 1907, the facility was equipped to host the National Trophy Rifle and National Trophy Pistol Matches and NRA National Rifle and Pistol Championships, together known as the National Matches.

Named for Commodore Oliver Hazard Perry, the victorious American commander who defeated the British at the Battle of Lake Erie during the War of 1812, Camp Perry quickly became a useful center for offering marksmanship training to meet deficiencies that arose during the Spanish-American War of 1898. By 1909, the facility had grown into a permanent camp featuring the largest and best-equipped rifle and pistol ranges in the world.

In addition to serving the needs of Ohio's adjutant general, Camp Perry has also played a vital role in federal service. During World War I, the facility was used as a training center for officers and marksmanship instructors. The Adjutant Erie Ordnance Depot west of Camp Perry was used to support weapons testing and development for the war effort.

During World War II, Camp Perry also served as a reception center for new recruits and as the prisoner of war facility described in this book. Some of the original hutments constructed for housing the prisoners are still standing as of this writing. New barracks and modern residential facilities have now replaced the huts and are used for housing troops and are open to the public as well—much like a state park—before, during and after the National Matches.

Today's Camp Perry is a blend of military and law enforcement preparedness, history and recreational use by the public. The Civilian Marksmanship Program (CMP), a nonprofit organization dedicated to firearms safety and marksmanship with an emphasis on youth, provides many marksmanship-related programs and is responsible for overseeing the National Matches. The CMP's program division is headquartered at Camp Perry.

Evidence of Camp Perry's early days remains today, thanks to historic preservation efforts. The outdoor rifle and pistol ranges still occupy virtually the same footprint they did in 1907. Brick and mortar structures, like "Commercial Row" used during the National Matches, served as mess halls for troops before and after World War II and by prisoners of war. Today, they house sport shooting vendors and accessories dealers during the matches.

The north water tower, used today only as an aid to navigation, was a common landmark during World War II. The redbrick National Guard buildings 1, 2 and 3, and the Camp Perry Chapel—all built in the 1930s by the Works Progress Administration—have been carefully maintained and remain substantially the same as they were during the war. Many new

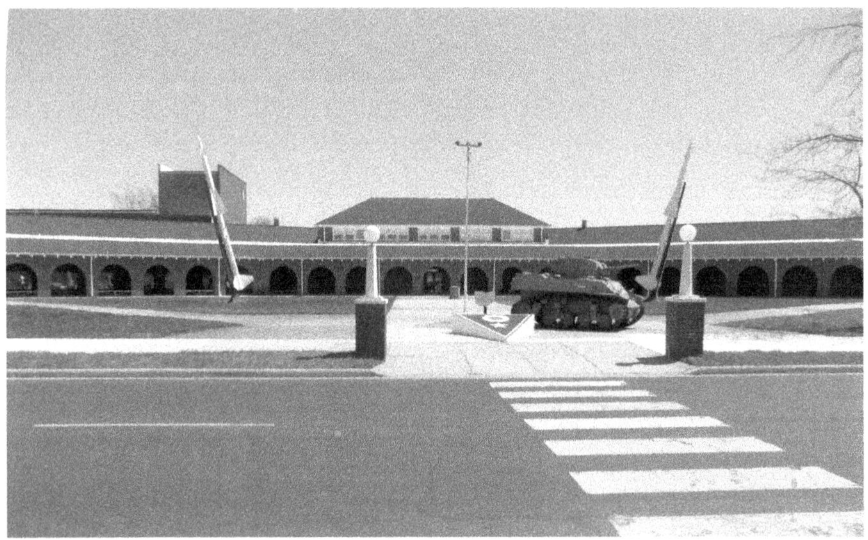

EPG Administrative Center when the POWs were on-site. *Courtesy of author's Camp Perry photo collection with the approval of the Ohio National Guard and Camp Perry Joint Training Center.*

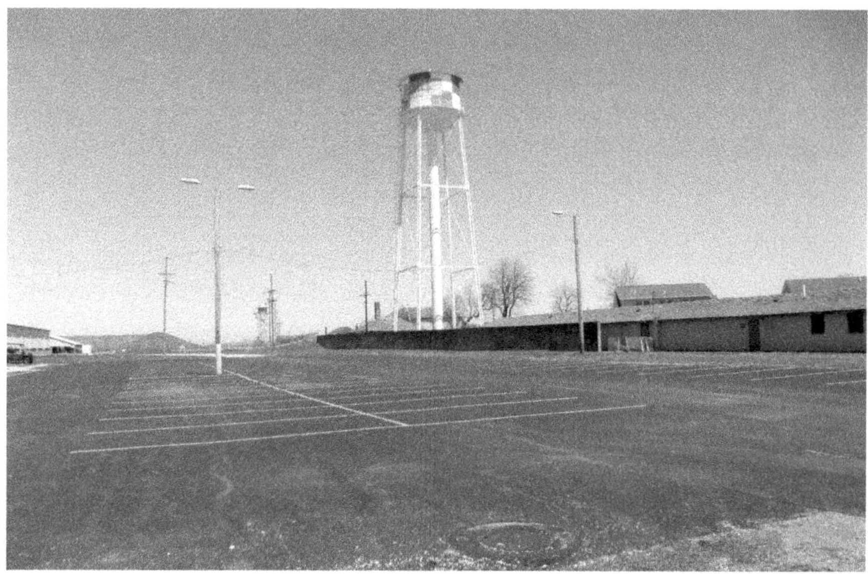

EPG Water Tower still in existence since World War II. *Courtesy of the author's Camp Perry photo collection with the approval of the Ohio National Guard and the Camp Perry Joint Training Center.*

buildings, barracks, classrooms and improved marksmanship ranges have been added to the current six-hundred-acre complex.

Camp Perry is an open state facility and welcomes visitors. Lodging and a fully equipped recreational vehicle park are available for rent throughout the year, with limited vacancies during the busy National Matches period in July and August. A sandy public beach and fishing pier near the lodging areas are open most of the year. Located six miles west of Port Clinton, Ohio, Camp Perry is a unique and enjoyable place to visit for anyone who appreciates the outdoors, Ohio history and, of course, marksmanship.[247]

Camp Perry and its branch camps during World War II were major contributors to alleviating the labor shortages on area farms and private industries. Lieutenant Colonel E.C. McCormick Jr., the Camp Perry commandant, announced on September 22, 1944, that the branch camps had generated money for the federal government through contracts with firms and farmers totaling $70,000 for Bowling Green, $45,000 for Celina and from $50,000 to $60,000 for Defiance.[248]

Despite Germany's defeat on May 7, 1945—which marked the celebration of Victory in Europe Day (V-E Day)—the prisoners of war in the United States were still fulfilling a robust role in meeting the labor shortage in private industries and farms throughout the country. Labor at the hands of German and Italian prisoners of war at Camp Perry and its branch camps had netted more than $2 million in revenue for the federal government, according to an announcement by McCormick on August 3, 1945. The revenue contribution was made possible due to the 1.5 million man-hours of prisoner of war labor that was already completed since January 1945. Another statistic indicated that German prisoner of war labor was responsible for picking more than 900,000 pounds of cherries as of August 1945, according to one report from W.W. Wilder, a cherry grower in Clyde, Ohio. At the Erie Proving Ground, meanwhile, the work of ISU members saved more than $300,000 in salvaging materials.[249]

It is clear that the prisoners of war who were housed at Camp Perry and its branch camps helped to satisfy the crucial labor needs of both the private industries and farmers in the Ohio region and were major revenue contributors to the federal government. Yet despite Camp Perry's beneficial impact on the region's economy, the camp and its surrounding operations also left lasting scars on the health of local residents and the environment that is still being remediated today. A continued effort is underway to clean up the land on which Camp Perry operated and on which it oversaw the production and disposal of a great quantity of ordnance that, while integral to helping win the war, was also detrimental to the health of local residents and the environment.

It is just one of the many contradictions found in the rich history of Camp Perry, from the first Italian prisoners of war who arrived at the camp, who were known for their affable, easygoing natures, to their successors, the German prisoners of war, who were remembered for their seriousness and, sometimes, intractability; from the local residents who recall fondly their intermingling with the prisoners of war, working alongside them, and even their chance reunions later in life, to those who held the prisoners of war in disdain because they felt they were being coddled by the government and were unfairly given brand-name foods while they as American citizens struggled with day-to-day needs; from the danger sign currently on display warning the public to keep out to avoid the toxic contamination, to the year-round opening of Camp Perry's doors to the public to enjoy recreation and firearms training. Camp Perry, the Erie Proving Ground and its branch camps remain a study in contradictions.

APPENDIX A

ACKNOWLEDGEMENT OF RECEIVING A GIFT

HEADQUARTERS
PRISONER OF WAR CAMP
Camp Perry, Ohio

Dear:

I wish to acknowledge receipt of your gifts to be used solely for the benefit of the Italian Prisoners of War. Rest assured that all gifts have been placed at the disposition of the prisoners and are being used by the entire group.

Italian prisoners at this camp are being treated very humanely. They do not lack food, shelter, nor clothing. The greater number are sent to work daily on various types of details such as carpentry, plumbing, masonry, harvesting, and cultivating on nearby farms.

One question which I know is on the lips of each person is the thought that perhaps a brother, son, relative, or friend may be among our group. Due to the War Department restrictions it is impossible for this office to relay any information on this subject, however, if the name of the person is submitted to the Prisoner of War Information Bureau at Washington, D.C. the desired information will be forwarded to you.

May I again express my sincere gratitude for the numerous and lovely gifts which we have received. My only wish is that each of the Prisoner of War could personally and individually thank you.

Very truly yours,

E.C. McCormick, Jr.,
Major, Infantry,
Commanding
PWCP Form No. 22

Contract No. W33-069 pgm 280

APPENDIX B

ENGLEBECK LABOR CONTRACT

Camp File No. 280

CONTRACT FOR PRISONER OF WAR LABOR
WAR DEPARTMENT

PRIISONER OF WAR CAMP: CAMP PERRY, OHIO:
CONTRACTOR: Harry Engleback

ADDRESS: Route 1, Port Clinton, Ohio

LOCATION AND DESCRIPTION OF PROJECT: Farm, 4 miles East of Port Clinton, Ottawa County on the Put-in-Bay Auto Ferry Road. Picking produce.

AMOUNT: $2,000.00

WAR MANPOWER COMMISSION CERTIFICATE is attached, number ....

dated 9/1/44

This contract is authorized by and has been negotiated under Public No. 354, 77th Congress, and Executive Order No. 9001.

DISTRIBUTION

1. Original signed number—General Accounting Office.
2. Duplicate signed number—Provost Marshall General.
3. Triplicate signed number—Contractor.
4. Authenticated copy—Retained by Commanding, Prisoner of War Camp.
5. Authenticated copy—Commanding General of the Fifth Service Command.
6. Authenticated copy—State Director, War Manpower Commission.

APPENDIX C

ENGLEBECK BILLING STATEMENT

ARMY SERVICE FORCES
Fifth Service Command
Prisoner of War Camp
Camp Perry, Ohio

25 September 1944

THE UNITED STATES TO:
Harry Engleback, Route #1 Port Clinton, Ohio
For Prisoner of War Labor furnished as follows:
Period: 6 September 1944 to 9 September 1944 Inclusive

Contract No. W33-069 pmg 280 Dated 1 September 1944 Proj. No. 278

Location of Project: Farm 4 miles East of Port Clinton, Ohio

NO. PW	RATE OF PAY	MAN HR WKD	AMT DUE	TR ALLOW	BAL DUE
10	$.50 per hr.	310	$155.00	$7.92	$147.08

In accordance with existing regulations payment should be made directly to this headquarters
by certified check, Cashier's Check or Postal Money Order made payable to THE TREASUER
OF THE UNITED STATES in the amount of
One hundred forty-seven dollars and eight cents

One signed copy of this bill must accompany remittance.

I certify the above to be a true and correct statement and the amounts shown hereon to be in accordance with the records of this organization.

By Robert Engleback

(Title)

Note: All remittance and any correspondence pertaining thereto, should be addressed to COMMANDING OFFICER, Prisoner of War Camp, Camp Perry, Ohio.

Partial Billing

APPENDIX D

ENGLEBECK TRANSPORTATION BILLING

Port Clinton Coach Lines
301 West Second Street
Port Clinton, Ohio
Phone 8081

To Mr. Engleback
Harbor Road
Port Clinton, Ohio

Date September 13, 1944

Sept. 6 Hauled 11 prisoners.	$4.40
Sept. 7 " " "	$4.40
Sept. 8 " " "	$4.40
Sept. 9 " " "	$4.40
Total:	$17.60

NOTES

Introduction

1. Lewis and Mewba, *History of Prisoner of War*, 90–91.
2. Benard, et al., *The Battle Behind the Wire*, 8.
3. Ibid., 15.
4. Lewis and Mewba, 90–91.
5. Ottawa County Historical Museum, *Camp Perry Photographs*.
6. Gansberg, *Stalag: U.S.A.*, 72.

Chapter 1

7. Lewis and Mewha, *History of Prisoner of War*, 90–91.
8. NARA, *Map of Prisoner of War Camps*.
9. Lewis and Mewba, 121.
10. Ibid, 91.
11. NARA, *Iron Cross, Second Class*.
12. NARA, *German POW Officers Waiting*.
13. NARA, *German POWS Boarding the Train*.
14. NARA, *German POW Officers Aboard a Train*.
15. Lewis and Mewba, 149.
16. NARA, *PMGO Inspection Reports–Perry*, 1943.
17. Ottawa County Historical Museum, *POW Camp Photographs*.

18. Ibid.
19. Ibid.
20. Lewis and Mewba, 154.
21. Ibid., 154.
22. Listman, et al., *Historic Context*, 4.6.
23. Ibid., 4.6.
24. Krammer, "German Prisoners of War," 70.
25. Ansbacher, "Attitudes of German Prisoners of War," 17.
26. Headquarters, Army Service Forces. *Handbook for Work of Supervisors*, 17.
27. Ibid., 10.
28. Ibid., 15.
29. Ibid., 17.
30. Listman, et al., 7.5.
31. Lewis and Mewba, 107.
32. Ibid., 108.
33. Ibid., 121.
34. Gansberg, *Stalag: U.S.A.*, 28.
35. NARA, *German POWs Taking Draftsmanship*.
36. Ottawa County Historical Museum, *Camp Perry Photographs*.
37. Listman, et al., 7.18.
38. Lewis and Mewba, 107.
39. Listman et al., 7.23.
40. Ibid., 7.22.
41. Lewis and Mewba, 100.

Chapter 2

42. NARA, *Other Inspection Reports*, February 8, 1943.
43. NARA, *PMGO Inspection Reports*, 1943.
44. *Port Clinton Herald and Republican*, October 1, 1943.
45. Ibid., October 8, 1943.
46. Ibid., October 16, 1943.
47. Ottawa County Historical Museum, *Camp Perry Photographs*.
48. *Port Clinton Herald and Republican*, October 16, 1943.
49. *Ottawa County News*, May 12, 1944.
50. Ottawa County Historical Museum, *Camp Perry Photographs*.
51. *Ottawa County News*, May 16, 1944.
52. Ibid., May 26, 1944.

53. Ibid., June 2, 1944.
54. *News Herald and Republican*, June 2, 1944.
55. *Ottawa County News*, July 7, 1944.
56. Ibid.
57. Ibid., September 8, 1944.
58. Ibid., November 2, 1944.
59. Ibid., August 3, 1944.
60. Ottawa County Historical Museum, *Camp Perry Photographs*.
61. *Ottawa County News*, September 22, 1944.
62. NARA, various photographs.

Chapter 3

63. *Ottawa County News*, May 11, 1945.
64. NARA, *Historical Report—Erie Proving Grounds*, 10.
65. Ibid., 14.
66. Van Keuren, *Erie Proving Ground Photographs*.
67. Ottawa County Historical Museum, *Camp Perry Photographs*.
68. *Beacon*, "The History of Erie Gardens," 1.
69. Ottawa County Historical Museum, *Camp Perry Photographs*.
70. NARA, *Historical Report—Erie Proving Grounds*, 10.
71. U.S. Army Corps of Engineers, Louisville District, 1.
72. Ohio EPA, 1.
73. U.S. Environmental Protection Agency, *Handbook on the Management of Munitions Response Actions*, 1.
74. Van Keuren, *Erie Proving Ground Photographs*.
75. Ibid.

Chapter 4

76. NARA, *Italian Prisoners of War in the Hospital*, October 19, 1943.
77. NARA, *Other Inspection Reports*, January 13–15, 1944.
78. Cooper, *Camp Perry Photographs*.
79. Van Keuren, *Camp Perry Photographs*.
80. Ibid.
81. NARA, *PMGO Inspection Reports–Perry*.
82. Ibid.

83. Ibid.
84. Van Keuren, *Erie Proving Ground Photographs.*

Chapter 5

85. NARA, *PMGO Inspection Reports–Perry: Memorandum 12*, November 2, 1943.
86. Ibid., *Memorandum 11*, November 1, 1943.
87. Ibid., *Memorandum 4A*, October 12, 1943.
88. Ottawa County Historical Museum, *Camp Perry Photographs.*
89. NARA, *Memorandum 6*, October 14, 1943.
90. NARA, *PMGO Inspection Reports–Prisoner of War Camp Perry, Form #22.*
91. NARA, *Memorandum 10*, October 27, 1943.
92. NARA, *Other Inspection Reports—Perry*, February 27, 1944.
93. Ibid., February 13, 1945.

Chapter 6

94. NARA, *Memorandum 8*, October 14, 1943.
95. Alfred Dymann letter to home.
96. Cooper, *Camp Perry POW Letter*, July 17, 1944.
97. Cooper, *Camp Perry POW Postcard*, February 8, 1944.
98. NARA, *Memorandum 8*, 1943.
99. Ibid.
100. Ibid.
101. Ottawa County Historical Museum, *Camp Perry Photographs.*

Chapter 7

102. NARA, *Other Inspection Reports—Perry*, February 27, 1944.
103. Ibid., October 6, 1944.
104. Van Keuren, *Camp Perry Photographs.*
105. New York Public Library, *Der Aufbau*, December 15, 1945.
106. NARA, *Other Inspection Reports—Perry*, January 13–15, 1944.
107. Ibid., February 27, 1944.
108. Ibid., January 23–24, 1945.

109. Ibid., February 13, 1945.
110. U.S. Army War College Library, *Der Aufbau*, October 6, 1945.
111. New York Public Library, *Der Aufbau*, December 8 and 15, 1945.
112. Ibid., December 15, 1945.
113. Ibid.
114. Cooper, *Camp Perry Photographs*.
115. Ottawa County Museum, *Camp Perry Photographs*.
116. NARA, *POWs Playing Cards*.
117. Van Keuren, *Camp Perry Trench Art*.
118. Frank, *Camp Perry POW Coupon Book*, 2017.
119. NARA, *Inspection Report*, February 13, 1945.
120. Ottawa County Museum, *Camp Perry Photographs*.
121. Ibid.
122. NARA, *Memorandum 9*, October 23, 1943.

Chapter 8

123. *Ottawa County News*, June 30, 1944.
124. *Port Clinton and Republican*, August 18, 1944.
125. *Toledo Blade*, July 3, 1944.
126. *Ottawa County News*, July 21, 1944.
127. Ibid.
128. *Ottawa County News*, August 18, 1944.
129. Ibid.
130. *Toledo Blade*, October 5, 1944.
131. *Toledo Blade Sunday Times*, March 16, 1975.
132. *Inspection Report*, February 27, 1944.
133. Ibid., October 6, 1944.
134. Ibid., January 23–24, 1945.
135. Ibid., February 13, 1945.
136. *Ottawa County News*, July 11, 1945.
137. *Der Aufbau*, December 15, 1945.

Chapter 9

138. NARA, *Memorandum 7*, October 14, 1943.
139. NARA, *Memorandum 240/3*, January 4, 1944.

140. *Port Clinton Herald and Republican,* October 1, 1943.
141. *Ottawa County News*, February 11, 1944.
142. Ibid., May 12, 1944.
143. Ibid., November 2, 1944.
144. *Port Clinton Herald and Republican,* June 2, 1944.
145. *Ottawa County News,* July 7, 1944.
146. Ibid., September 8, 1944.
147. Ibid., January 19, 1945.
148. Ibid., August 3, 1945.
149. NARA, *Inspection Report*, August 17, 1945.
150. NARA, *Memorandum*, October 13, 1944.
151. Ottawa County Historical Museum Englebeck Contracts & Billings.
152. Ibid.
153. Ibid.
154. Ottawa County Historical Museum, *External Contract Details*, April 11, 1945.
155. NARA, *Camp Peery POW Strength Report,* January 14, 1944.
156. NARA, *Shortage Prisoner of War*, April 23, 1945.
157. *Toledo Times*, September 18, 1945.
158. *Ottawa County News*, February 15, 1946.

Chapter 10

159. *Ottawa County News,* July 28, 1944.
160. *Toledo Blade*, September 2, 1944.
161. NARA, *Inspection Report–Defiance*, October 5, 1944.
162. Ibid.
163. *Defiance Crescent News*, September 2, 1944.
164. NARA, *Time Schedule Active Work Projects*, April 9, 1945.
165. Buchman, *Correspondence*, November 2, 2017.
166. NARA, *Inspection Report–Celina*, October 5, 1944.
167. Ibid.
168. Ibid.
169. Ibid.
170. *Daily Standard,* January 17, 1974.
171. *Toledo Blade*, September 26, 1944.
172. *Daily Standard,* January 17, 1944.
173. BGSU, *Lease of Land*, April 1, 1945.

174. NARA, *Inspection Report-Bowling Green*, October 5, 1944.
175. Ibid.
176. Bowling Green State University, *Conclusion of POW Camp Lease.*
177. Fisher, *Wilmington POW Camp.*
178. Fisher, *Wilmington POW Camp Photo.*
179. Ibid.
180. Ibid.
181. Fisher, *German POW Experience.*
182. Banks, *Map of Crile General Hospital Photo.*
183. NARA, *Other Inspection Reports–Perry.*
184. Banks, *POW Quarters.*
185. Fletcher General Hospital Postcard.
186. NARA, *Return to: General Reference & Research Branch*, 1945.
187. NARA, *Other Inspection Reports–Perry.*
188. NARA, *Return to: General Reference & Research Branch*, 1945.
189. NARA, *POW Labor Report*, January 31, 1946.
190. NARA, *Return to: General Reference & Research Branch*, 1945.
191. Booth, "Remembering the Army's Fletcher General Hospital."
192. NARA, *Other Inspection Reports–Perry*, 1944–1945.
193. Whitehall Historical Society, *Columbus ASF Depot POWS*, 1940s.
194. NARA, *Other Inspection Reports–Perry.*
195. Ibid.
196. *Old Fort News.*
197. Ibid.
198. Ibid.
199. Ibid.
200. Mosher and Mosher, *Scioto Ordnance Plant*, 83.
201. Ibid., 72.
202. U.S. Army Corps of Engineers, *Scioto Ordnance Depot.*
203. Department of Defense, *Defense Environmental Programs*, 80.
204. NARA, *RG 389, Entry 461*, 1944–45.
205. Mosher, 83.
206. Rossford Public Library, *Photo of the Rossford Ordnance Depot.*
207. Toledo-Lucas County Public Library, *Photo of Jeeps at the Rossford Ordnance Depot.*
208. *Toledo Blade*, November 1, 1944.
209. *Toledo Times*, August 16, 1944.
210. Department of Defense, *Defense Environmental Programs*, 78.

Chapter 11

211. Gansberg, *Stalag: U.S.A.*, 51.
212. *Ottawa County News*, July 21.
213. Ibid., March 2, 1945.
214. Ibid., March 9, 1945.
215. *Marion Star*, March 9, 1945.
216. *Ottawa County News*, June 1, 1945.
217. Ibid., August 31, 1945.
218. *Port Clinton Herald and Republican*, August 25, 1944.
219. *Ottawa County News*, October 5, 1945.

Chapter 12

220. U.S. Army War College Library, *Der Aufbau*, October 6, 1945.
221. *Ottawa County News*, May 11, 1945.
222. New York Public Library, *Der Aufbau*, December 15, 1945.
223. Ibid.
224. U.S. Army War College Library, *Der Aufbau*, October 6, 1945.
225. New York Public Library, *Der Aufbau*, December 8, 1945.
226. U.S. Army War College Library, *Der Aufbau*, October 6, 1945.
227. Ibid.
228. New York Public Library, *Der Aufbau*, December 15, 1945.
229. Ibid.
230. New York Public Library, *Der Aufbau*, December 8, 1945.

Chapter 15

231. U.S. Army Corps of Engineers, *FUDS Inventory*.
232. U.S. Government Accounting Office, *Ohio FUDS Cleanup Program*.
233. Pavwlik, "Eire Army Depot."
234. Ohio EPA, *Erie Army Depot*.
235. U.S. Army Corps of Engineers, *Former Marion Engineer Depot*.
236. Ibid.
237. Ibid.
238. *Columbus Dispatch*, "Leukemia News Stuns Marion."

239. *Marion Star*, "River Valley Graduates and Families We Need Your Help," February 8, 1999.
240. U.S. Government Accounting Office, *Ohio FUDS Cleanup Program.*
241. Pawlik, "Erie Army Depot."
242. *Columbus Dispatch*, May 31, 2017
243. U.S. Army Corps of Engineers, *Proposed Plan Incendiary Fuel Disposal Area.*
244. U.S. Government Accounting Office, *Ohio FUDS Cleanup Program.*
245. Department of Defense, *Defense Environmental Restoration Program.*
246. Ibid.

Chapter 16

247. Cooper, *Camp Perry Today*, 2017.
248. *Ottawa County News,* September 22, 1944.
249. Ibid., August 3, 1945.

BIBLIOGRAPHY

American Psychological Association: Washington, D.C. Distributed by www.Forgottenbooks.com.

Ansbacher, H.L. "Attitudes of German Prisoners of War: A Study of the Dynamics of National-Socialistic Fellowships." *Psychological Monographs: General and Applied* 62, no. 1 (April 10, 1948).

Banks, James. *Map of Crile General Hospital Photo*. Crile Archive Center for History Education. Parma, OH: Cuyahoga Community College–Western Campus, 2017.

———. *POW Quarters*. Photo No. 2012.23.2. Crile Archive Center for History Education. Parma, OH: Cuyahoga Community College–Western Campus, 1945.

Beacon (OH). "The History of Erie Gardens." February 23, 2017. Ottawa County Historical Museum, Port Clinton, Ohio.

Benard, Cheryl, et al. *The Battle Behind the Wire—U.S. Prisoner and Detainee Operations from World War II to Iraq*. Santa Monica, CA: RAND National Defense Research Institute, 2011.

Booth, Richard. "Remembering the Army's Fletcher General Hospital." *Now & Then Magazine*. Wooster, OH: Spectrum Publications (August 2017).

Bowling Green State University, Center for Archival Collections. *Conclusion of POW Camp Lease of Land*. November 16, 1945.

———. *Land Lease Between the City Bowling Green, Ohio and the Ohio Agricultural Extensive Service for a POW Camp*. April 1, 1945.

Buchman, Randall. *Teenage Boy Working with German POWs* (correspondence). November 2, 2017.

City of Bowling Green, Ohio, and the Ohio Extension Service. *Land Lease*. Bowling Green, OH: 1945.

Columbus Dispatch. "Leukemia News Stuns Marion." FOIA P1L021.0312, Department of the Army, U.S. Army Corps of Engineers, Louisville, Kentucky, October 17, 1997.

Cooper, Steve. *Camp Perry Photographs*. North Civilian Marksmanship Program, Camp Perry Training Site, Port Clinton, Ohio, 2017.

———. *Camp Perry POW Letter, July 17, 1944*. North Civilian Marksmanship Program, Camp Perry Training Site, Port Clinton, Ohio, 2017.

———. *Camp Perry POW Postcard, February 8, 1944*. North Civilian Marksmanship Program, Camp Perry Training Site, Port Clinton, Ohio, 2017.

———. *Camp Perry Today*. North Civilian Marksmanship Program, Camp Perry Training Site, Port Clinton, Ohio, 2017.

Daily Standard (OH). "From Burial Ground to Camp for War Prisoners." January 17, 1974. Ohio State University Extension, Mercer County, Celina, Ohio.

Defiance Crescent News. "Demand for Prisoners' Work May Keep Camp in Defiance Throughout Winter." September 26, 1944. Defiance, OH: Andrew L. Tuttle Memorial Museum.

Department of Defense. *Defense Environmental Programs Annual Report to Congress for FY 2014*. Office of the Under Secretary of Defense for Acquisition, Technology, and Logistics, Washington, D.C., September 2015.

———. *Defense Environment Programs Annual Report to Congress for FY 2015*. Office of the Under Secretary of Defense Acquisitions, Technology, and Logistics, Washington, D.C., September 2016.

———. Defense Environmental Restoration Program. Table 7, 37. Retrieved from https://www.denix.osd.mil/derp/archives/progress/fy2015tables, 2015.

Dymann, Alfred. *German Prisoner of War Letter Sent Home to Family, February 4, 1945*. Purchased at www.ebay.com.

Englebeck Labor & Billing Contracts. Ottawa County Historical Museum, Port Clinton, Ohio, September–October, 1944.

Fisher, Kay. *The German POW Experience in the United States and Wilmington, Ohio*. Wilmington, OH: Clinton County History Center, 2017.

———. *Wilmington Camp*. Wilmington, OH: Clinton County Historical Center, 2017.

———. *Wilmington POW Camp Photo*. Wilmington, OH: Clinton County Historical Center, 2017.

Fletcher General Hospital Postcard in the 1940s. Purchased from www.stores.ebay.com/sdguyer.

Frank, Dave. *Camp Perry POW Coupon Book*. 2017. Retrieved from www.worldandmilitarynotes.com/pow/camp-perry-ohio-usa-pow-camp.

Gansberg, Judith M. *Stalag: U.S.A.—The Remarkable Story of German POWs in America*. New York: Thomas Y. Crowell Company, 1977.

Headquarters, Army Service Forces. *Handbook for Work of Supervisors of Prisoners of War*. M 811. Washington, D.C.: U.S. Government Printing Office, July 1945.

Krammer, Arnold P. "German Prisoners of War in the United States." *Military Affairs* 40, no. 2 (April 1976): 68–73. Retrieved from http://www.jstor.org.

Lewis, George G., and John Mewha. *History of Prisoner of War Utilization by the United States Army 1776–1945*. Department of the Army Pamphlet, No. 20-213: Department of the Army, Washington 25, D.C. U.S. Government Printing Office, June 24, 1955.

Listman, John, Christopher Baker and Susan Goodfellow. *Historic Context: World War II Prisoner-of-War Camps on Department of Defense Installations*. Project Number 05-256. Department of Defense Legacy Resource Management Program. Washington, D.C., July 10, 2007.

Mosher, Charles D., and Delpha R. Mosher. *The Scioto Ordnance Plant and the Marion Engineer Depot of Marion, Ohio—A Profile After Forty Years*. Glanz Printing Company, Wauseon, Ohio, 1987.

National Archives and Records Administration. *German POWs Boarding a Train*. Photo No. SC 197674-s. College Park, Maryland, 1944.

———. *German POWs Grinding Meat at Camp Perry*. Photo No. 208-AA-310-F-3. College Park, Maryland, August 21, 1944.

———. *German POW Officers Aboard a Train*. Photo No. SC 197675-s. College Park, Maryland, 1944.

———. *German POW Officers Waiting to Receive Valuables*. Photo No. SC 197679-s. College Park, Maryland, 1944.

———. *German POW Preparing Meals at Camp Perry*. Photo Number No. 208-AA-310-F-6. College Park, Maryland, August 21, 1944.

———. *German POW Stirring Soup at Camp Perry*. Photo No. 208-AA-310-F-1. College Park, Maryland, August 21, 1944.

———. *German POW Taking Down Meat at Camp Perry*. Photo No. 208-AA-310-F-5. College Park, Maryland, August 21, 1944.

———. *German POWs Taking Draftsmanship*. Photo No: 208-AA-3092-2. College Park, Maryland, 1945.

———. *Historical Report–Eire Proving Grounds, Lacarne, Ohio–Third Quarter*. Box 8. Chicago, Illinois, 1945.

———. *Iron Cross, Second Class Being Removed from Prisoner's Blouses*. Photo No. SC 197669-s. College Park, Maryland, 1944.

———. *Italian Prisoners of War in the Hospital at Camp Perry, Ohio*. Photo No. 111-SC-387222. College Park, Maryland, October 19, 1943.

———. *Map of Prisoner of War Camps*. Records of the Office Provost Marshal General. (Record Group 389). Subject Correspondence files. Entry Al 435. College Park, Maryland, April 1, 1945.

———. *Other Inspection Reports–Perry*. RG 389, Entry 461. Box 2669 @ Stack Location 290/34/28/5. College Park, Maryland, 1944-1945.

———. *PMGO Inspection Reports–Perry: Memorandum's 1–21*. RG 389, Entry 461. Box 2669 @Stack Location 290/34/28/5. College Park, Maryland, 1943.

———. *PMGO Inspection Reports–Prisoner of War Camp Perry Form (PWCP Form Nos.)*. RG 389, Entry 461. Box 2669@ Stack Location 290/34/28/5. College Park, Maryland, 1943.

———. *POWs Playing Cards*. Photo No. 111-SC-387222. College Park, Maryland, October 19, 1943.

———. *Prisoner of War Camp Labor Report—Fletcher General Hospital, Cambridge, Ohio*. SPVID 319.1. College Park, Maryland, January 31, 1946.

———. *Return to: General Reference & Research Branch—The Historical Unit, U.S. Army Medical Service*. Forest Glen Section, Walter Reed Army Medical Center, Washington, D.C. Administration, College Park, Maryland, 1945.

———. *Shortage Prisoner of War–Fifth & Sixth Service Commands*. RG 211 Entry 175. College Park, Maryland, April 23, 1945.

———. *Time Schedule Active Work Projects: Defiance POW Camp*. College Park, Maryland, April 9, 1945.

New York Public Library. *Der Aufbau*. Interlibrary and Document Services. New York, December 8 and 15, 1945.

Ohio EPA. *Erie Army Depot*. Site Number: G050H0027. Retrieved from epa.ohio.gov/portals/30/FFS/docs/fuds/Erie_Army_Depot.pdf.

Old Fort News. "'A By-Product of War'—A History of Camp Thomas A. Scott, 1942–1949." 49, no. 2 (1986). The History Center, Fort Wayne, Indiana.

Ottawa County Historical Museum. *Camp Perry Photographs*. Port Clinton, Ohio, 1940s.

———. *Englebeck Contracts and Billings*. Port Clinton, Ohio, 1944.

———. *POW Camp Photographs*. 1940s.

———. *Suggested Instructions to Contractors Under Contract for Prisoner of War Labor*. Port Clinton, Ohio, 1944.

Ottawa County News. "Army Cancels Italian Tour of Sandusky—Congressman Jumps War Dept. for 'Pampering' of Italian Service Units." July 21, 1944. Ida Rupp Public Library, Port Clinton, Ohio.

———. "Bread & Water Diet Is Ordered for Prisoners." March 2, 1945. Ida Rupp Public Library, Port Clinton, Ohio.

———. "Camp Perry to Close Next Wed. as Army Post." February 15, 1946. Ida Rupp Public Library, Port Clinton, Ohio.

———. "'Date Hut' Is Innovation at E.P.G. Village—Hut Provides Homey Place for Villager Ladies to Entertain Guests." August 18, 1944. Ida Rupp Public Library, Port Clinton, Ohio.

———. "Find Escaped Perry Prisoner Hanging in Tree." October 5, 1945. Ida Rupp Public Library, Port Clinton, Ohio.

———. "Former Italian Prisoners Not Replacing Civilians." May 26, 1944. Ida Rupp Library, Port Clinton, Ohio.

———. "German Prisoner Eludes Stockade." August 31, 1945. Ida Rupp Public Library, Port Clinton, Ohio.

———. "German Prisoners Arrive at Camp Perry—Italian Group Is Transferred." June 2, 1944. Ida Rupp Public Library, Port Clinton, Ohio.

———. "German Prisoners at Camp Perry Were Not Surprised at Surrender—Now They Were Not Talk More Freely, Camp Commander Says." May 11, 1945. Ida Rupp Public Library, Port Clinton, Ohio.

———. "German Prisoner's Escape Is Reported." June 1, 1945. Ida Rupp Public Library, Port Clinton, Ohio.

———. "Germans Quit Strike, Go Back to Jobs Monday." March 9, 1945. Ida Rupp Public Library, Port Clinton, Ohio

———. "Italian Battalion Is Activated at EPG." May 12, 1944. Ida Rupp Public Library, Port Clinton, Ohio.

———. "Italian Group Taken on Tour of Port Clinton—Officers Greatly Impressed by Visit to Places of Interest in Local Area." June 30, 1944. Ida Rupp Public Library, Port Clinton, Ohio.

———. "Labor of German and Italian Prisoner Based at Perry Has Netted the Government Over $2,000,000 in Revenue to Date." August 3, 1945. Ida Rupp Public Library, Port Clinton, Ohio.

———. "Nazi Prisoner Are Rationed Too, News Reporters Learn." September 22, 1944. Ida Rupp Public Library, Port Clinton, Ohio.

———. "New Prisoners from Normandy Arrive at Camp Perry Only 21 Days After the Invasion of France—Reporters Touring Camp See Old and New Prisoners Exchange Greetings." July 7, 1944. Ida Rupp Public Library, Port Clinton, Ohio.

———. "1000 Prisoners Arrive Friday at Camp Perry—New Group, All Navy Men; Sent Here to Provide More Farm Labor." August 3, 1945. Ida Rupp Public Library, Port Clinton, Ohio.

———. "Perry Receives More Germans—Arrival of 'Several Hundred' More Prisoners Announced Last Friday." January 19, 1945. Ida Rupp Public Library, Port Clinton, Ohio.

———. "Perry Receives More Prisoners – Several Hundred Arrived Yesterday Direct from Battle Area in France." September 8, 1944. Ida Rupp Public Library, Port Clinton, Ohio.

———. "Plan Transfer of Italian Units at Camp Perry—To Be Sent to Rossford Ordnance Depot, Toledo, Within the Coming Week." November 2, 1944. Ida Rupp Public Library, Port Clinton, Ohio.

———. "Post-War Role Is Slated for Proving Ground." May 11, 1945. Ida Rupp Public Library, Port Clinton Ohio.

———. "Sit-Down Strike Nets Germans Bread & Water." July 21, 1944. Ida Rupp Public Library, Port Clinton, Ohio.

———. "Teach English to Germans PW's at Camp Perry—Classes Being Conducted to Teach Language and Am. History to Prisoners." July 13, 1945. Ida Rupp Public Library, Port Clinton, Ohio.

Pawlik, Eugene. "Erie Army Depot & Marion Engineer Depot." Email. September 16, 2018.

Port Clinton Herald and Republican. "Excellent Job Performed by Italian Units—Commanding Officers at Erie Proving Ground Perry Praise ISU Efforts." August 18, 1944. Ida Rupp Public Library, Port Clinton, Ohio.

———. "Gracia, Americans!—Italian Prisoners Happy at Camp Perry; Have Own Mascot." October 16, 1943. Ida Rupp Public Library, Port Clinton, Ohio.

———. "Italian Prisoners Join Allied War—Organized into Military Units at Camp Perry." May 12, 1944. Ida Rupp Public Library, Port Clinton, Ohio.

———. "Italians Transferred to Other Section—Will Be Available for Gardening and Food Processing Work in This Area." June 2, 1944. Ida Rupp Public Library, Port Clinton, Ohio.

———. "Italian War Prisoners—Give New Quarters 'Going Over' on Arrival Sunday." October 8, 1943. Ida Rupp Public Library, Port Clinton, Ohio.

———. "Perry Named Italian Prisoner of War Camp: Will Put Them at Contract Jobs." October 1, 1943. Ida Rupp Public Library, Port Clinton, Ohio.

———. "Prisoner's Death Is Believed a Suicide." August 4, 1944. Ida Rupp Public Library, Port Clinton, Ohio.

Rossford Public Library. *Photo of the Rossford Ordnance Depot, WW II.* Rossford, Ohio, 2018.

Marion Star. "POWs on Strike." March 2, 1945. Marion, Ohio.

———. "River Valley Graduates and Families We Need Your Help." FOIA P1L021.0239, Department of the Army, U.S. Army Corps of Engineers, Louisville, Kentucky, February 8, 1999.

Toledo Blade. "Cradle of Postwar Democracy for Italians Being Carved at Erie Proving Ground—Captives War Enjoying Freedom in Simplest Form." October 5, 1944. Local History and Genealogy Department, Toledo Lucas County Public Library, Toledo, Ohio.

———. "Italians Admire Museum's Statuary. Former War Prisoners Tour City." July 3, 1944. Local History and Genealogy Department, Toledo Lucas County Public Library, Toledo, Ohio.

———. "Italians in Ohio Worried About Homefolk—Prepare Their Own Spaghetti and Get Adequate Quarters." October 29, 1943. Local History and Genealogy Department, Toledo Lucas County Public Library, Toledo, Ohio.

———. "Where Is Our Lather? Nazi PWs Getting Fat on GI Chow, Medical Officer Says." September 26, 1944. Local History and Genealogy Department, Toledo Lucas Public Library, Toledo, Ohio.

Toledo Blade Sunday Magazine. "Toledo Was a Nice Place to Be a Prisoner." March 16, 1975. Local History and Genealogy, Toledo Lucas County Public Library, Toledo, Ohio.

Toledo-Lucas County Public Library. *Photo of Jeeps at the Rossford Ordnance Depot.* Local History Department, Toledo, Ohio, 2018.

Toledo Times. "Italian Work Units Labor at Rossford." August 16, 1944. Local History and Genealogy, Toledo Lucas County Public Library, Toledo, Ohio.

———. "Last PWs Leave Toledo Industries." September 18, 1945. Local History and Genealogy, Toledo Lucas County Public Library, Toledo, Ohio.

U.S. Army Corps of Engineers. *FUDS Inventory.* Retrieved from http://www.usace.army.mil/Missions/Environmental/Formerly-Used-Defense-Sites.

U.S. Army Corps of Engineers, Louisville District. *Erie Army Depot.* 2009–2010. Retrieved from http://www.lrl.usace.army.mil/Missions/Environmental/Erie-Army-Depot.

———. *Former Marion Engineer Depot River Valley Expanded Site Inspection.* December 2001. Retrieved from www.lrl.usace.army.mil.

———. *Proposed Plan Incendiary Fuel Disposal Area (SOP-Z), Former Scioto Ordnance Plant, Marion, Ohio.* January 30, 2015. Retrieved from www.lrl.usace.army.mil.

———. *Scioto Ordnance Depot.* 2012. Retrieved from http://lrl.usace.army.mil/Missions/Environmental/Scioto-Ordnance-Plant.

U.S. Army War College Library. *Der Aufbau.* U.S. Army Heritage and Education Center, Carlisle, Pennsylvania, October 6, 1945.

U.S. Environmental Protection Agency. Interim Report. *Handbook on the Management of Munitions Response Actions.* Washington, D.C.: Office of Solid Waste and Emergency Response, May 2005.

U.S. Government Accounting Office. *Ohio FUDS Cleanup Program.* July 31, 2001. Retrieved from https: www.gov/gao.gov/gao-01-1012sp/OH.html.

Van Keuren, James P. *Camp Perry Photographs.* Port Clinton, Ohio, 2017.

———. *Camp Perry Trench Art Photographs.* Port Clinton, Ohio, 2017.

———. *Erie Proving Ground Photographs.* Port Clinton, Ohio, 2018.

Whitehall Historical Society. *Prisoners of War Working at the Columbus Depot.* Whitehall, Ohio, 2017.

INDEX

P

R

S

T

W

Y

ABOUT THE AUTHOR

Dr. James Van Keuren, Ed.D., is retired professor of educational administration and dean of the Dwight Schar College of Education at Ashland University in Ashland, Ohio, where he published numerous juried journal articles, as well as a book entitled *Web-based Instruction: A Practical Guide for Online Courses.* Prior to Ashland University, Dr. Van Keuren was a teacher, high school principal, school superintendent and assistant and interim state superintendent of public instruction in Ohio. His most recent book, *A Tribute to the 109th Evacuation Hospital (SM)*, traces his father-in-law's service during World War II. Dr. Van Keuren has been married to his wife, Pat, for forty-eight years, and they have daughters Michelle Scott and Christie Murdoch, in addition to grandchildren Hailey Scott, Weston Murdoch and Cooper Murdoch.

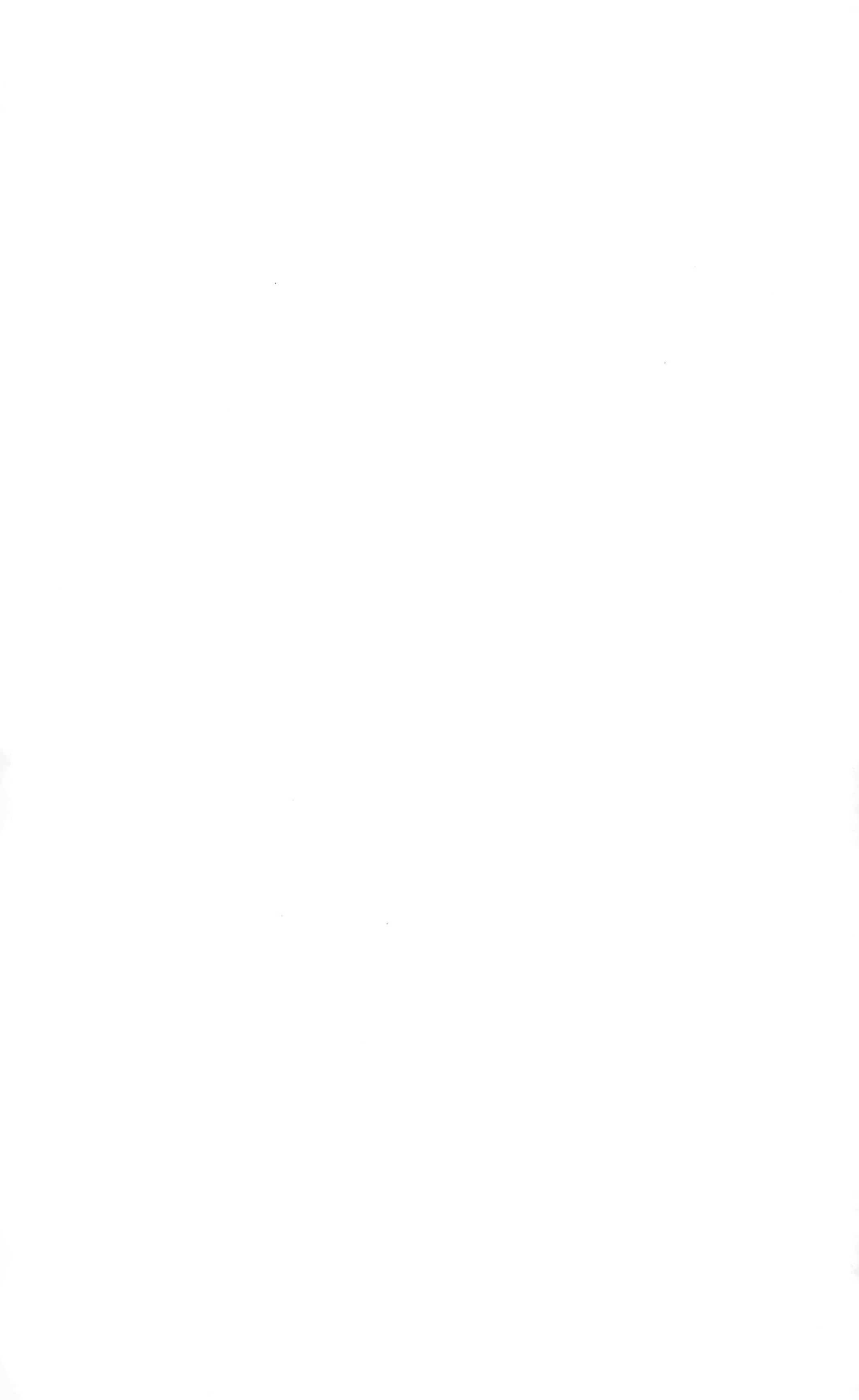

www.ingramcontent.com/pod-product-compliance
Lightning Source LLC
LaVergne TN
LVHW052337100826
845147LV00020B/1090

* 9 7 8 1 4 6 7 1 4 1 6 6 6 *